1,001
WAYS TO *Relax*

1,001 WAYS TO Relax

An Illustrated Guide to Reducing Stress

MIKE GEORGE

CHRONICLE BOOKS

SAN FRANCISCO

1,001 Ways to Relax
Mike George

First published in the United States in 2003
by Chronicle Books, LLC.

Conceived, created, and designed
by Duncan Baird Publishers.

Library of Congress Cataloging-in-Publication
Data available.

ISBN 0-8118-4165-0

Manufactured in Singapore

Typeset in Shannon

Editors: Lucy Latchmore, Hanne Bewernick
Assistant editor: Emily Mason
Managing designer: Manisha Patel
Designer: Rebecca Johns
Commissioned artwork: Trina Dalziel,
Emma Harding, and Debbie Lush

Distributed in Canada by Raincoast Books
9050 Shaughnessy Street
Vancouver, British Columbia V6P 6E5

10 9 8 7 6 5 4 3 2 1

Chronicle Books LLC
85 Second Street
San Francisco, California 94105

www.chroniclebooks.com

CONTENTS

INTRODUCTION

Just as it takes all kinds of people to make our world so various and so beautiful, so too it takes many forms of relaxation to create rest and renewal at each level of our being and in each area of our lives.

I have to confess that when I first set out to think about *1,001 Ways to Relax*, the thought occurred to me, "This is absurd, there's no way there are 1,001 ways to relax." However, it wasn't long before I realized there are probably tens of thousands of ways. And all of these methods differ from each other in time, place and depth – by which I mean that there is a vast difference between, on the one hand, relaxing for a few minutes in order to free ourselves from the physical and mental tensions that we accumulate in the average day; and, on the other hand, years of practising the deepest forms of spiritual relaxation, in the manner recommended by the sages and the saints. And there is an equally huge gap between relaxation that relieves a few stressful symptoms and ways that reach deep inside the soul and heal the core causes of our spiritual discomforts.

During the process of creating and gathering material for this compendium of tools, tips and techniques I have been reminded time and time again how the simplest of changes at the level of our thoughts, perceptions and actions can release us from our anxieties. I believe that what makes this little book a special companion is that it truly contains remedies, rescues and exercises for almost every commonplace situation and any moment of our waking lives. From the home to the workplace, from early morning to late evening, from our relationships with others to our very important relationship with ourselves, you will find literally hundreds of ideas to experiment with.

Twenty years of researching stress and helping others to understand, manage and prevent this totally curable condition have brought home to me the overwhelming fact that everyone has different needs at different times. That's why, in this mini-compendium, you'll find methods that address the tensions in your body, techniques to deal with sadness, guilt and other disturbing emotions, visualizations to help you transform old patterns of negative thinking, and meditations to give you access to the deepest dimensions of spirit. For it is, of course, deep in the soul that we will always find the most natural and eternal calm.

There are many ways to use this little book. You could spend a week or two working through a specific section, trying out the most relevant techniques and noting down others for experiment some time in the

future. You could focus on one area of your life that is not as relaxed as you would like it to be, and you could work with the index and contents pages to find specific ways to help you change. Alternatively, you could dip in and out, and enjoy the delights of serendipity as you give yourself the gift of a new way to relax every day. And if you decide to do one of the most relaxing things in life, which is to give a gift to a friend, then why not become what you might call a "benevolent adviser" by pointing out to the person who will be fortunate enough to receive this book from you the three numbered exercises that you recommend they read first, simply because you sense that this is what would help them most.

Don't be fooled by the obvious simplicity of some of the suggestions. You may be surprised to discover how the smallest of actions can trigger the greatest rewards. And don't miss one of the underlying threads of the book: the reminder that ultimately "being" comes before "doing" in the lexicon of relaxation. True, everything you do will have an effect on your state of being; but more importantly, when you learn to create your state of being, when you can establish peace in your heart, invoke love in your relationships and donate happiness to everyone around you, then you will know that your spirit is as relaxed and as joyful as it can ever be.

We live in tense, turbulent and, for many people, unrelaxing times – of that reality there is no doubt. But we can easily avoid adding to the turbulence. In fact, we can become one of those people for whom the world has a great need: those who can stay calm in a crisis, cool in the midst of chaos, and focused on the positive when all around are inclined to reinforce the negative. If we can stay relaxed and calm, this helps others to do the same. If we can always respond with a positive note, we help others stay in tune with the symphony of life. If we can keep seeing life through optimistic eyes, we can brighten someone else's day in a single second! In all these ways we do much more than maintain a calm state of being within ourselves: we radiate outward an extremely positive energy, and in so doing we serve the world.

Mike George
(mike@relax7.com)

Mornings

WAKING WELL

1   **Wake up naturally,** without an alarm clock, at least once a week if you can. This will help you reconnect with your bodily cycles (or circadian rhythms, to use the scientific term). Note that going to bed an hour earlier will not necessarily bring forward your natural waking time by an hour – you may find that you lie awake, worrying that you can't sleep. If your circadian rhythms make you a night owl at heart, go with the flow and have a weekend lie-in when you need one. If you're a lark, spring out of bed when the time seems right – you may find there's time before breakfast to do some worthwhile meditation.

2   **Let sunlight wake you** through open curtains or shades. If the light floods in early, **use the extra time gained (3)** to plan the day, prepare for it mentally, or do an exercise routine.

4   **Let music wake you.** Set the timer on your CD-player to wake you with a piece that starts very quietly and either continues in that vein or builds up slowly to a higher volume. Try the overture to Wagner's opera *Das Rheingold*, whose

swirling opening bars segue into a wake-up dawn chorus by the Rhinemaidens. As an alternative you could put on an Indian raga specifically created for morning playing – there are plenty to choose from, and they always begin with a moody slow movement performed on sitar or sarod without percussion.

5   **Draw insights from dreams** in the morning while they are still fresh. We cannot confirm the truth of dream symbolism, as the unconscious runs no helpline. But if, in a spirit of adventure, we start to explore possible meanings of dreams, we can usually arrive intuitively at constructive insights, which heighten self-awareness and feed into our subsequent tranquility.

    Why not keep a dream diary (6) in which to record your dreams so that you can review them later in the day? Writing them down will help to free you from any anxieties of the night, leaving you ready to face the day in a positive frame of mind.

7   **Immediately on waking,** "think how you can give joy to at least one person today." These are the words of the nineteenth-

century philosopher Friedrich Nietzsche – a surprising person to have come up with such an uplifting thought, as he is more often associated with deeply skeptical, angst-ridden philosophy.

8 **Use a dimmer switch** in the mornings to increase light levels by stages – so that your day starts gently.

9 **Enjoy the symphony of noise** that penetrates your bedroom – the traffic outside, the birdsong, the jackhammers, the news on your neighbour's radio. Don't let extraneous noises stress you, just because you aren't in control of them. Instead, imagine that all these sounds are a wonderful random concert for which you have a privileged free ticket. Listen mindfully. Enjoy each cacophonous moment.

10 **Engage all five senses** each morning, as soon as you awaken. The sight of sunlight, the sound of birdsong, the feel of a towel, the taste of fruit juice, the smell of toast – check off each sense in turn as the brain-signals flood in.

STARTING THE DAY

11   **Throw open a window** to start the day with deep drafts of air and blow away the cobwebs that have settled on your well-rested spirit in the night. Even if you've had a window part-way open all night, this is a good way to get the air circulating freely. Don't let bad weather put you off – rain or snow can be just as refreshing for the spirit as brilliant sunshine.

12   **Close your eyes** for a whole minute, and imagine you were born without the gift of sight. Open your eyes and let the world flood your senses. Then imagine your "higher senses" opening to bring you an intense experience of all the world's beauty. After your imaginary act of sense deprivation you will no doubt feel a corresponding gratitude. Try to keep a sense of that gratitude with you as the effect of your minute's darkness fades.

13   **Say a morning prayer** in three stages: first give thanks for the new day; then, for other people, wish for health and happiness; and finally, for yourself, pray for (or aspire to) the qualities that will equip you best for the coming day.

Confirm your prayer through action (14). For example, send a card or make a phone call to one of the people you prayed for – someone who you believe needs your support right now.

15   **Do a pre-dawn meditation.** In many spiritual traditions the first meditation of the day takes place between 4 and 5 am. It is during this period that the atmosphere is at its most peaceful and free from distraction. This makes it the easiest time to meditate and spend quality time with yourself – what better way to calibrate your energies for the day ahead?

16   **Meditate on your breath** immediately after getting out of bed. As you breathe in, keep your chest still and push out your abdomen – as if you were blowing up a balloon in your stomach. As you breathe out, drop your shoulders and imagine yourself squeezing out air, as though pressing water out of a sponge. Do this for ten complete breaths. As you do so, feel the energy of the new day enter your body.

17   **Go for a pre-breakfast walk,** to enjoy the sights and sounds of the early morning and work up a healthy appetite.

18   **Watch a spider spinning** its web. Treat the web like a mandala (a sacred diagram used in meditation: see page 112). Focus on the intricate concentric pattern as it develops. As you appreciate its complexity and beauty, be aware of the web's dual existence – out there in the world as well as an impression in your mind. Allow the image to hang in your perception, just as the web itself hangs in empty space.

19   **Enjoy the half-light of dawn** – the way in which colours fill out the shapes you see, gradually displacing the grayness.

20   **Celebrate sunrise on the shortest day** of the year (21st December in the northern hemisphere) – a worthwhile ritual of the spirit. The winter solstice, as this day is known, is a reminder that even during the dreariest months the life-force remains strong. Devise your own simple ceremony for the occasion – perhaps a candlelit breakfast, or an early morning tea ceremony using herbal tea. In addition, you might choose to add a golden star, an emblem of the sun, to your Christmas tree decorations. In summer, **sunrise on the longest day (21)** (21st June in the northern hemisphere: the summer solstice) is a symbol of nature at her most magnificent. Your ceremony might include a meditation on a flower (see point 252, page 115), perhaps making a garland of flowers for a loved one, and a prayer of thanks for the many hours of daylight you can enjoy together.

22 **Imagine six impossible things before breakfast,** like the White Queen in Lewis Carroll's surreal fable, *Alice in Wonderland*. This activity primes the mind to expect the unexpected, and deal with it in a calm, accepting manner. To get you in the mood, here are two examples: a country where clockmakers are arrested for mistreating time; a reclusive hermit

who believes that he can love his fellow men and women more purely and intensely from an uninhabited island.

23   **Shower in the morning, bathe in the evening.** Each time of day has its own natural mood or energy. If we attune our daily activities (in this case our bathing rituals) to the fluctuating rhythms of the day, we will feel an indefinable sense of "rightness".

24   **Sing in the shower.** Singing has its roots in the innate happiness of the spirit, reminding us of our true nature. It is also a celebration of the interfusion between body, mind and soul. As you sing, allow the vibration to begin in your heart, fill your body and then the room – it's good to be alive!

25   **Put on a bright shirt** and add a splash of colour to your day. Your very presence will liven up the environment for those around you! Each colour has a symbolic significance. Pick one that resonates particularly with your mood or your goals that day: red is associated with courage and passion; yellow with sunlight and optimism; blue with openness and calm; green with tranquility and balance; white with purity and spiritual peace.

If a conservative dress code operates in your workplace, remember that there's nothing to stop you wearing **a brightly coloured tie or necklace (26)** instead.

27   **Wear your new skirt (or jacket) today,** don't save it for a special occasion – today *is* a special occasion.

28   **Wear something amusing** under your clothes – such as, a witty phrase on a tee-shirt. This underlines that there's more to all of us than is apparent from our surface appearances. Indeed, the true path of the spirit often leads us away from commonly accepted norms.

29   **Wear white** if you feel like it – even white trousers, or a white skirt. There's something charismatic about white clothes. Affirm to yourself beforehand that you aren't going to worry about marks – if they happen, they happen.

30   **Wear clothes that fit.** Well-fitting garments are not only more comfortable but they also look better, improving our self-esteem and body-image. Don't be tempted to buy something that almost fits, just because you're bored with shopping!

   Wear fabrics that appeal to your sense of touch (31), such as soft, cozy wool, or smooth, luxurious velvet.

   Wear natural fabrics (32), such as cotton and linen, which allow your skin to breathe, thereby minimizing skin irritations.

33   **Look for things** you've misplaced if you end up with spare time in the morning. There's always something whose precise whereabouts you're not able to pinpoint. Don't worry if you can't find it: you may well make unexpected discoveries during your search. Be willing to be sidetracked. This is free time.

34   **Drink fresh fruit juice for breakfast.** This will provide you with a concentrated supply of vitamins, minerals, enzymes and other nutrients that will enhance your body's immunity and general well-being.

     Invest in a juicer (35) so that you can make your own juices. Because they are entirely fresh and unprocessed, home-made juices are more nutritious than store-bought versions. They also offer scope for producing more permutations of flavours.

     Cleanse and refresh (36) your body from the inside out with the juice of three apples, one bunch of red grapes and one nectarine. **Banish colds (37)** and kick-start the immune system with a zingy combination of three apples, two carrots and half an inch (1 cm) of ginger root – rich sources of antioxidants.

38   **Have a smoothie** for breakfast. Pulped in a blender rather than juiced in a juicer or citrus press, smoothies provide a more filling, slower-releasing alternative to juices. This is because, unlike juices, smoothies contain fibre, which slows digestion and the absorption of nutrients, as well as mobilizing the gut.

Chase away winter blues (39) with a sun-drenched taste of the tropics in a blend of one banana, half a pineapple, half a papaya and eight tablespoons (120 ml) of guava juice. **Ward off morning hunger-pangs (40)** with a filling, energy-rich smoothie comprising two bananas, eight rehydrated prunes, three drops of vanilla essence, five tablespoons (75 ml) of natural yogurt and six tablespoons (90 ml) of pineapple juice.

41 **Limit yourself to one coffee** in the morning – if you can't break the habit entirely. Consumed in excess, coffee over-stimulates the adrenal glands, leaving you irritable and nervy, and causes dehydration by acting as a diuretic.

Experiment with caffeine-free coffee substitutes, such as **chicory (42)**, **dandelion (43)** and **Californian coffeeberry (44)**. If you can't find these ready-prepared in the stores, make your own with the roots of chicory or dandelion, or the seeds of Californian coffeeberry. In each case, let the roots or seeds dry before roasting, grinding and then percolating them like ordinary coffee grounds.

45   **Always eat breakfast.** The traditional wisdom of enjoying a breakfast fit for a king and reducing the size of subsequent meals throughout the day, culminating in a pauper's dinner, is well judged. A generous breakfast kick-starts your metabolism, sets you up for the day, and replaces lost fuel after the night's "fast".

46   **Enjoy a porridge breakfast** – oats provide a sustainable source of energy to get a winter day off to a good start and are also rich in B vitamins, which help to keep you calm.

For a summery alternative to porridge, try **Bircher muesli (47)** – packed with nutrients, this was the original muesli recipe, concocted by Dr Bircher for the patients at his clinic in the Swiss mountains. Soak a handful of oats in water or unsweetened fruit juice overnight (to render them more digestible). Combine the soaked oats with one grated apple, a handful of chopped dried or fresh fruits, a handful of chopped nuts or seeds, and two tablespoonfuls of natural yogurt or sweetened condensed milk.

48   **Forget yesterday's mistakes.** Today is a new day, your mind has been refreshed by sleep, and there is no need to believe that yesterday's misjudgments or misfortunes will repeat themselves. Make yourself a checklist of all that you have learned from past mistakes – and now move on.

49   **Imagine a robber** has visited you in the night and made off with all your past experiences and ingrained habits, but you have a magic spell that brings back everything you assent to. You are, for the moment, free of any burden you choose not to accept. Today, whatever happens, you have the awareness to select an appropriate response, rather than reacting automatically. See what it feels like – for a while – to be the person you wish to be.

50   **Decide to be happy** today, no matter what happens or who does what. It is within your power to make this leap. Happiness is the true condition of the self-aware, and its source lies within ourselves. To decide to be happy is a positive, self-fulfilling action, comparable to "I do" in a marriage ceremony.

51   **Create a personal affirmation** and declare it twenty times
to yourself each morning. Affirmations are simple, positive "I am
…" statements (such as, "I am at peace," "I am a tower of
strength") that build self-esteem and a strong sense of self. They
counter the negative messages that we often give ourselves by
reminding us of our intrinsic value. In your affirmation include
those qualities that you readily recognize in yourself, as well as
those you are prospecting for.

    If you are having difficulty recognizing your strengths,
ask a friend (52) what positive qualities they see in you.
Include these in your affirmation. Create **specific affirmations
(53)** to prepare you for days that you know will be particularly
challenging. Cover the qualities that will be most helpful to you
when coping with the day's events.

54   **Plan ahead.** The morning is a good time for planning,
because you'll be feeling fresh and positive. Think in particular
about what you will need to buy or borrow to carry out your
projects. Set aside time to carry out these preparations.

Plan for any difficult situations (55) that the day is likely to hold. Think of the qualities you expect to need – for example, focus and concentration for an intellectual task, tact and diplomacy for difficult people, an attitude of acceptance for potential disappointments. Decide whether you're likely to need more of any quality than you'll be able to summon naturally and impromptu. If so, plan to allow time before the event to collect yourself and meditate into existence the required qualities from your innermost reserves.

56   **Call yourself from home** before setting off for work in the morning and leave a message on your work voicemail – perhaps a reminder to yourself of some treasured insight, a resolution for the day ahead, or perhaps even a joke to drive away morning blues.

Do this for someone else (57) – perhaps a friend or family member who is not enjoying their work at the moment – to sound a positive note as soon as they arrive at the workplace.

OFF TO WORK

58 **Transform your journey to work** into quality time with yourself by using the opportunity for reading, listening to music or low-key meditation. (If you travel by public transport, you may need to leave home earlier, to be sure of a seat.)

Alternatively, use the time to **pay attention to your surroundings (59)**, soaking up the sights and sounds of the people and places you encounter on your journey. You could even **engage someone in conversation (60)** – outrageous though this suggestion may sound!

61 **Walk the pretty route** to work if there is one – if this necessitates a detour, bear in mind that the exercise is good for you.

62 **Close your eyes** and think of the crowds as a communion of souls enjoying the shared experience of travel. Feel the warmth of humanity around you. Rejoice in the contact.

Give up your seat (63) to someone who needs it more than you. You will be surprised how good this simple act of kindness makes you feel.

64 **Do a sardine meditation** in a crowded train. You are surrounded by strangers. Imagine that you are all sardines, packed together in one small tin. Rather than resenting those around you, you recognize that essentially you are all alike in nature and share the same predicament. This will give you a sense of fellow-feeling with all the other commuters.

65 **Walk mindfully to your workplace,** noticing what is going on around you. This will give you accurate local knowledge, and you may make some useful discoveries. In particular, check out the local cafés and look for new establishments opening up where one day you might choose to meet a friend or hold an informal business meeting.

66 **Have breakfast** with a friend, a short walk from your workplace. Early morning meetings, when the mind is alert and you feel positive about the day ahead, can be very productive.

67 Look up at the rooflines as you walk to work – often there are many wonderful features high above your head, especially in the older cities where different architectural periods and styles jostle together.

68 Enjoy a shoe-shine on your way to work, whether mechanical or assisted. (New York is the great shoe-shine capital of the world, but the service is spreading.) Afterwards, give a respectful nod to your reflection in your newly polished footwear.

69 Give someone a lift if you drive to work. A friendly conversation in the morning can put you in a good mood for hours – and you have the added comfort of helping to reduce the levels of greenhouse gases in the atmosphere.

Arrange for four drivers (70) to take it in turns to ferry the other three.

71 **Car essentials** – furnish your car with useful accessories such as a map, an umbrella, a pair of sunglasses, a box of tissues, a torch, and a cloth to wipe your hands if you have a breakdown and need to fiddle with the engine.

If you live in an extreme climate, **be prepared for adverse weather (72)**: in cold climates supplies of food and water in the car are desirable, in addition to warm clothes and a shovel for clearing snow.

Dealing with stress and emotions

— QUICK FIXES

73 **Visualize a blue bubble** stretching protectively around your body. Blue is associated with protection and tranquility. Imagining ourselves enveloped in this blue film helps to prevent our energies from being leached by those around us. This technique is particularly useful when we feel stressed by crowds.

Alternatively, **draw a circle of protection around yourself (74)**. Imagine a circle being drawn around you on the floor or ground, then imagine invisible, impregnable but totally transparent walls rising from the circle to protect you. You are invulnerable: nothing can touch the essential self whose dominion is the invisible tube you have placed around yourself.

75 **7/11 breathing** is a simple technique for dealing with the sharp, shallow breaths resulting from an agitated mental state. Breathe in slowly and steadily to the count of seven; then breathe out slowly and steadily to the count of eleven. Continue with this rhythm of in-breaths and out-breaths until your breathing becomes more relaxed and regular and the tension that triggered your anxiety begins to subside.

76   **Lay your head on a pillow** or cushion to release anger and tension. Imagine it's a sponge sucking and absorbing all the tensions and frustrations out of your mind, like blotting paper, from which they evaporate into the air.

77   **Squeeze a stone in your hand** as hard as you can; then gradually release your fist. Rock the stone gently as if making peace with it. Do this every time you feel stressed or angry, until the feelings drain away.

78   **Press your palm** in the centre with the thumb of your other hand to relieve nervousness in stressful situations, like exams and interviews. Increase the pressure steadily as you breathe out. Hold for 3 to 7

seconds. Release the pressure as you breathe in. Repeat three
times or until you feel the anxiety begin to dissipate.

79   **Be Pavlovian.** The Russian scientist, Ivan Pavlov, discovered
that the body can be trained to react on cue whenever a
particular stimulus is given. Try exploiting this effect to induce a
sense of inner calm during moments of stress. First you need to
put Pavlov's principles into practice. Whenever you are feeling

happy and relaxed, recall an event in your life that gave you pleasure, and at the same time pinch one of your earlobes. If you do this often enough, you will unconsciously come to associate earlobe pinching with the physiological state of relaxation. This technique equips you with a means to combat the physical symptoms of stress: in theory, when you pinch your earlobe, your stress levels should diminish automatically, as your brain remembers its training.

80 **Try stress ballooning.** Imagine loading your worries into the basket of a hot-air balloon. In your mind's eye, untie the ropes that hold down the balloon and watch it rise. Your problems become more remote as the balloon disappears into the clouds.

81 **Sing away sadness.** It doesn't matter how well you can sing. Expressing yourself through song releases pent-up emotion, lifts the spirits and helps to reconnect you with a sense of life's endless possibilities.

82 **Breathe out a negative, breathe in a positive.** This exercise involves placing a particular imaginative interpretation upon your breathing. Sit comfortably and allow your body to relax. Now focus your attention on your breath. As you breathe out, visualize the negative emotion, such as anger, streaming out of your nostrils; as you breathe in, imagine an appropriate emotion, such as compassion, being drawn into your lungs and from there into your bloodstream, where it is carried to every part of your body. Continue this exercise, exhaling anger and inhaling compassion, for about 5 minutes.

Other variations of this exercise include: **breathe out blame, breathe in understanding (83)**; **breathe out resentment, breathe in acceptance (84)**; **breathe out revenge, breathe in forgiveness (85)**.

86 **Don't just do something, sit there!** Contrary to the usual exhortation, this is sometimes the best approach when emotions are running high, your problems seem insurmountable, or your intuitive compass is not giving you a clear direction to follow.

Simply take a few moments to sit in stillness, gathering your strength. Give your mind and body permission to relax.

87 **Roll Chinese meditation orbs** together in the palm of your hand to encourage a calm, alert state of mind. Allow the repetitive movements of your hands and the hypnotic clicking sound of metallic orbs to soothe you. Relish the mental stimulation afforded by this dextrous action.

88 **Drip cold water onto your wrists** whenever you are feeling hot and bothered. Cooling the wrists has a refreshing effect on the whole body because it is here that arteries (large blood vessels that distribute blood throughout the body) are found close to the surface.

To achieve a similarly refreshing effect, **splash a little cold water behind your earlobes (89)**.

90 **Recall a smile** on the face of someone who loves you, to give you the strength to deal with problems. (If you find it difficult to picture their face clearly, you might find it easier to visualize a photograph of them instead.) Respond with a smile of your own and watch the smile of your loved one broaden further.

91 **Overcome party nerves** by imagining you are all taking part in an elaborate game of manners for the entertainment of an outside observer.

Alternatively, imagine that **everyone you meet has a secret and incongruous hobby (92)**. For example, that suave young man makes origami flowers; while that formidably intelligent lady reads superficial romantic novels.

93 **Hold a baby** for a while if you have the opportunity. This grounding experience will put your troubles into perspective. Revel in the baby's burbling smile.

DIFFICULT CHOICES

94   **Seek the questions** initially, rather than the answers. When navigating your way through complex issues, avoid opting automatically for the obvious route. Seeking answers too soon may trap you inside fake or oversimplified assumptions.

95   **Use glove puppets,** one on each hand, to dramatize your inner conflicts – for example, between your masculine and your feminine sides, or between your creative right-brain and your logical left-brain. This is a fun therapeutic technique, favoured by gestalt practitioners and art therapists among others.

96   **Stick with plan A,** for as long as possible. Doubt will often creep into your mind when you are part way along a chosen path. Do not abandon the plan immediately. View your doubts as a test of your resolve and ride out the wobbles.

     If your course of action continues to feel wrong and the doubts keep returning, be prepared to **rethink your course of action (97)** and if necessary seek an alternative path.

98 **Try self-counselling** whenever you have a dilemma to resolve. Eyes closed, imagine your alter-ego sitting opposite you in a chair. What questions does your other self ask? What are the truest responses you can give? Listen to your alter-ego's advice. Do you trust it? If so, take heed: you'll hear no better!

99 **Take a step, any step.** Paralysis can set in when we spend too long agonizing over what to do next. The key is to take an action and listen for any positive or negative feedback – remembering that the absence of feedback is itself feedback. You can then use this information to adjust your course if necessary.

100 **Ask yourself** what the "youthful sage" within you would do whenever you have difficulty making a choice. The youthful sage is your childhood self – as children we tend to be more in touch with our intuition. When we grow older, many of us feel that this innate wisdom

becomes stifled by conditioning and experience. Consulting your childhood self is a way of reconnecting with your intuition, helping you to make a choice consistent with your true self.

101 **Fortify yourself with inner strengths** before tackling a problem. Mentally stocktake the qualities you take pride in, as well as past and present achievements. Feel yourself grow more powerful with every source of strength you add to your list.

Complement this approach by **fortifying yourself with blessings (102)** – for example, the love you receive from others, the beauty of the natural world, the food on your table.

103 **Unravel a problem.** Most problems have a number of strands tangled together, often in complicated ways. If it seems impossible to unravel the knot, make a start by trying to name each of the different strands. Draw them on paper, with a word or two alongside each separate line to label it. You may find that identifying the ingredients of the problem in this way leads to a breakthrough in working out a solution.

104 **Read a classic novel** – a diversion that is particularly useful when you find yourself obsessively analyzing a problem without reaching any solutions. The linear narrative structure of a traditional novel can help to shift your circular thoughts into more progressive patterns, subliminally priming you to move through your problems toward possible solutions.

105 **Solve it by walking.** This is a translation of a Latin proverb, *Solvitur ambulando*. Take a half-hour walk and allow yourself to be soothed by the rhythm of your steps. You may detect an "inner sieve" at work, bringing your lightest, happiest thoughts to the surface, allowing your heaviest thoughts to drop away.

106 **Just do something – anything.** Sometimes we become so caught up in our thoughts that we are unable to make any headway. It is as though we are lost in a city, endlessly driving around the same few blocks. Taking a break from your thoughts and doing a completely unrelated activity can sometimes be enough to free the blockage.

Routine chores (107), such as cooking and cleaning, or **repetitive activities (108)**, such as driving, knitting and sewing, are particularly helpful in loosening the grip of recurring thought patterns, because they engage the left-brain, leaving the right-brain free to pursue alternative, more creative thoughts.

109 **Sit on it.** If a problem doesn't have to be resolved immediately, it can sometimes help to sit on it for a while. Make a note in your diary to reconsider the problem at a later date. Put it to sleep until then and get on with other things. After a week or so you may find that the problem has solved itself or that your mind is clearer and more able to find a resolution.

110 **Write your worries down.** This simple action can reduce your attachments to your worries, putting them into perspective and freeing you to think about other things.

If you can't let them go, take time out to **address your worries (111)**. Find a peaceful spot where you are unlikely to be interrupted and write down your anxieties. What is the worst

that can happen? What is the best possible outcome? Decide on some actions you can take over the next few days to reduce the likelihood of a negative result.

112 **Don't try to resolve everything in a day.** Make a list of outstanding worries in the early evening, then just switch off and enjoy yourself for the remainder of the day. Difficult tasks are much better faced with fresh energy in the morning.

113 **Resolve dilemmas on paper** using two columns, For and Against, when you can't decide whether or not to pursue a particular course of action. List the pros and cons in the relevant columns, giving marks for their importance on a scale of 1 (not important) to 5 (very important). Add up the totals for each column to see which decision carries the day.

114 **Consult a friend** when making a difficult choice, to find out what they would do in your position. With a fresh perspective, they may be able to shed some light on your dilemma.

115 **Accept the inadequacy of reason** for solving certain problems. Although effective when applied to a practical problem, logical arguments tend to break down when it comes to less clear-cut emotional issues. In such cases you may need to seek an alternative approach (see point 116, below).

116 **Follow your intuition** when trying to decide whether a particular course of action is right or wrong. If you feel logic overruling your intuition, close your eyes and imagine the optimum course of action as a ball of light rising from your stomach and filling your mind with truth.

117 **Follow your conscience.** Where moral issues are concerned, this can be a good way to cut through the confusion engendered by the conflicting voices of the outside world.

118 **Seek help from others** with problems that have defeated your solitary efforts – as the Ethiopian proverb puts it, "When spiders unite, they can tie up a lion."

BREAKTHROUGHS

119 **Visualize a locked box** sitting on a table in front of you. You have the only key. Inside the box is an object which represents the solution to a current problem. Close your eyes, remind yourself of the problem, then see yourself opening the casket. What lies inside? What clues does it give you?

120 **Make a path through a dense jungle** in your mind when faced with seemingly impossible situations. This visualization will strengthen your belief in yourself and your capabilities, as well as your faith that a way will be found. Imagine you are sitting on the ground surrounded by impenetrable thickets, a cacophony of animal noises all around. From your place on the ground, you visualize a path opening up behind you. When the moment comes for you to stand up and turn around, there is the path exactly as you imagined it. As you walk forward, you leave the noise behind. You can feel the trees watching you, smiling at you, celebrating your courage.

121 See the light at the end of the tunnel. When problems seem hard to bear, this meditation will give you hope of better things to come. Close your eyes and imagine yourself in total darkness. After a few minutes visualize a spot of light in the distance. As you walk toward it, the spot grows gradually larger. Eventually the outlines of a tunnel become visible. Sunlight floods in, revealing the floor and walls of the tunnel. Beyond the entrance you see a verdant landscape. Step out into the sunlight and feel the warmth on your skin. Feel a sense of peace as you find yourself in the world once more.

122 Cross a bridge from problem to solution. In your mind, visualize the vivid embodiment of your problem situated on the bank of a river. Now begin to construct a bridge across the river to reach the other side. The bridge has five piers, each of which represents a quality that you will bring to the situation: identify these qualities. Now see yourself walking across the bridge. On reaching the other side, you discover an object. This represents a solution. What does it look like? What does it mean?

123   **The rule of three.** One way to be more thorough in what we do is to break down our actions into three phases. For example, if you want to forgive someone, there would be the genuine wish to forgive; the act of forgiveness itself (whether silent or spoken); then the follow-through. Try this one–two–three approach when you want to deal systematically with an issue.

124   **Blitz your phobias** by gradual acclimatization. This involves exposing yourself to the object or situation that you fear at increasing levels of intensity. Progress to the next level only occurs when comfort is achieved at the current level. For example, if you had arachnophobia (fear of spiders), you would begin by looking at a photo of a spider. When you felt comfortable with this you would look at a model spider, then a real spider several feet away, then a spider closer up ... and so on.

125 **Take a global perspective** on your problems to understand their true scale. Imagine that you are orbiting the Earth in a flying saucer. Satellites beam images on to your console screen from anywhere you choose: office workers streaming ant-like through the streets of New York; a fishing fleet off the coast of Iceland; dolphins diving playfully in the Atlantic; wild geese flying in formation across the desert plains of Africa. As you zoom in close to watch the activities of these creatures you become aware that each one forms an integral part of the web of life. Consider your problems in the context of this greater whole. Do they seem smaller by comparison? Perhaps easier to bear?

126   **Don't be a catastrophizer.** When forecasting events, there is often a temptation to fixate on worst-case scenarios in the name of being prepared. However, this approach usually causes unnecessary angst – things are rarely as bad as we expect. In such situations, take sensible precautions, but make it a rule not to preoccupy yourself with fears of imagined future disasters.

127   **Decouple your worries.** When worries are lumped together they can seem so overwhelming that your entire life becomes one big insurmountable problem. Instead, try separating out your worries so that you can deal with each one individually. When you do this, each worry seems smaller and as a result easier to understand and ultimately deal with.

128   **Retune your memories.** Look back over any memories from the past that continue to cause you emotional pain. Examine your story of what happened. Try to separate the factual events from your interpretation. Is there a more positive way that you can interpret these events? You may find that retelling the story from a different, more positive angle loosens the emotional hold of your original version.

129 Imagine yourself in a year's time. Ask yourself how important the feelings you have now will seem to you then. This is a particularly good way to deal with anger, but it can also work for other emotions such as jealousy and resentment. Remember that in reality problems seldom have the immutable shape in which we might imagine them.

130 Think of reasons why you can do something rather than why you can't – all it takes is a shift in your attitude. Once you have broken the negative logic of your thinking, you gain space in which positive approaches can incubate.

131 Take the optimistic approach. According to psychological research, optimists adopt a specific "explanatory style" when interpreting the events that happen to them, attributing positive events to their own abilities and seeing negative events as isolated instances of bad luck. This approach bolsters self-esteem and peace of mind, giving those who practise it greater resilience and ability to cope with difficult situations.

132 **Collect proverbs** or sayings that relate to stressful situations, and use them as stress-absorbers. For example, if someone you value at work has let you down, quote from Geoffrey Chaucer's *Canterbury Tales*: "If gold shall rust, what shall iron do?" Collect quotes for every difficult situation you are likely to encounter.

    Share your wisdom (133): when a friend is having a tough time, send them a card in which you've written a saying that will console them or give them strength.

134 **Rise above praise and blame** and find equanimity in all your enterprises. To seek praise is to be reliant on others for self-esteem, which leaves you vulnerable to their changing moods and opinions. However, if we fill up our own cup of self-worth we feel much stronger within ourselves, better placed to cope with life's uncertainties and challenges.

TAKING CHARGE

135 **Accept negativity.** Often we compound negative states of emotion by getting frustrated with ourselves for not being as calm and centred as we would like, which in turn only makes us feel worse. Rather than trying to beat yourself into a positive frame of mind, take the time to acknowledge exactly how you are feeling. See if you can find a neutral place within yourself to sit side by side with your emotions, without trying to push them away. You may find that this loving acceptance of your own feelings works as an antidote, tempering some of the pain.

136 **Take responsibility for your emotions.** Blaming others for "making" you feel a certain way leads to "victim consciousness". Remember, you have the freedom to choose how you react to the world around you. To believe otherwise is to give away your personal power.

137 **Release the worry animal.** Sometimes worry is a monkey, jumping around your mind,

filling your life with anxiety.
Sometimes it is an elephant,
which stands in front of you – a
huge obstacle that obscures your
vision. Identify an animal that
best symbolizes your worry and
then set it free by opening the
doors of its cage (our worries are
held captive by our minds). See
it walk, run, fly or swim away.

**138 Write a letter from your
calm self** to your worried self
if you feel in need of advice and
reassurance but there's no one at
hand to provide it. Be as practical
as you can. You may surprise
yourself how easily you can tap
into the calm voice inside.

139 Know your own emotions. When we are fully aware of our emotional reactions, and we understand where they originate from, we have much more choice about how to respond to the people and events in the world around us.

140 Slice off your buttons. We all create buttons within our personality. Anyone touching them sets off in us some emotional outburst or long, deep sulk. Ridding ourselves of buttons can take anything from a week to a lifetime. First, identify them, then take responsibility for them, then slice through the threads with a mental scalpel. Imagine your personality as a multi-buttoned shirt and jacket. Go to work. But don't rush it – the buttonless wardrobe isn't created overnight!

141 **Challenge your inner critic.** Many of us possess a critical inner voice that chips away at our self-esteem, undermining all our achievements, laughing at our mistakes. For every error or failing that you catch your critic berating you for, think of two positive qualities that outweigh it.

Animate your inner critic (142). To reduce the power of this critical voice, give it the form of an animated character – perhaps a hissing, green snake or a devilish little gremlin. Make the appearance and voice of the character as ridiculous as possible to undermine the authority of its words.

143 **Declare an amnesty for negative thoughts.** Whenever you have one, imagine that it's come to give itself up. Accept its surrender and send it on its way, taking care not to criticize it for existing in the first place.

144 **Move the mountain.** Above all, faith is the power that overcomes obstacles. Have faith in yourself and your abilities, and you will find the strength to perform miracles.

145 **Be the gatekeeper** of your own heart. Vigilantly check everything that passes through the gates in either direction. Open the gates to those who come in peace or love. Bar entry to anything that will disturb your inner peace. Open the gates to allow your heart to extend its caring touch. Close the gates to contain any impulses that may cause harm.

146 **Question the word "should".** Used about yourself, this word reflects pressures that you are allowing to influence your behaviour. Take a moment to become aware of these pressures: do you wish to give them governance over what you do? Used of others, the word "should" can denote a subtle attempt at control. Find a replacement before the word reaches your lips.

Banish "have to" (147). The phrase "I have to" implies a surrender of will to an outside force. Empower yourself by taking responsibility for your actions. Replace the words "I have to" with "I choose to". You always have a choice, however difficult it may be. Notice how this subtle shift in attitude affects your perception of what you are *choosing* to do.

TIME OUT

148 **Imagine a peace room** – an extra room in your own home, dedicated to inner peace. Visualize how you will decorate it. What colour will you use to make it peaceful? What objects will you place in it? What is their significance and where will they go? Finally, fill your room with the vibrations of peace. Go there in your mind whenever you need to be refreshed.

In the same way, **imagine a happiness room (149)**, prompting yourself with similar questions when visualizing it. Go there to gain strength from all your sources of happiness.

150 **Retreat to the green room.** In most television studios there is a place called the "green room". This is a quiet room in which actors can take time out from the glare of the spotlights on set. If you find yourself in a difficult situation, imagine that you are an actor on a television set. When the stress becomes unbearable, take advantage of your actor's privileges and head for the green room. In this quiet mental space, you can clear your mind of all thoughts for a while. Once you've regained your composure, return to the set and resume work.

151 Read to a child a story of their own choosing. Whether the book offers soothing tales of the antics of furry animals or an action-packed adventure story, it will transport both you and the child to another realm, away from the troubles of everyday life. Any lingering traces of negative emotion will soon be washed away by the child's innocent pleasure.

152 The ship of peace. Imagine you have a free day and you are standing in a port on the quayside. The ship of peace sails in from the sea to collect you. Once on board you see the gentle smiles on others' faces, feel the peaceful atmosphere everywhere on the ship. A whistle blows and the ship sets sail. Visualize the peaceful sights you come across on your voyage.

153 Visualize a scene of natural calm. It may include a lake set against a spectacular backdrop of

mountains, or perhaps a cluster of tall palm trees, rustling gently in a warm tropical breeze – whatever holds most meaning for you. Enjoy the feeling of peace this scene gives you. Choose one object from the scene, and whenever your inner calm is disturbed, summon this object to mind. It will evoke your scene of tranquility and all its associated feelings.

154 **The country called Relaxation** is very different from home. Imagine yourself arriving there. What would you see on disembarking from the plane and making your way through the capital to your hotel? How does everyone manage to be so relaxed in all they do? What attitudes or habits might make this possible for you? Now come home for a vacation. Bring the culture of this newly discovered country with you.

155 **Sail to a tropical island** as a venue for meditation. In your mind, visualize yourself rowing out to your chosen island from port, counting down from twenty with each pull of the oars. Feel your breathing become easier stroke by stroke. On the

count of zero you glide onto the beach of the island. Find a soft
spot to sit down on the warm sand and begin your meditation.

156 **Plan a trip to an exotic place** – you do not actually have
to go there. Taking a mental journey to an unknown place is an
escape from your daily routine and an invitation to the mind to
go beyond the mundane. Research details about your chosen
destination. Visualize the journey. What will it be like when you
arrive? What are the best sights on and off the beaten track?

Immerse yourself in a different culture (157). For
example, read about the Japanese way of celebrating a wedding, or the mysterious ways of the native American shamans.

158 **Use a map** to work out the farthest you can get from any
other human being within a day, morning or afternoon.
Make your way there, alone. Enjoy the privilege of your own
company. Relish the distance between yourself and your
sources of stress. Replenish your reserves of inner strength.

Alternatively, simply **imagine where you would go (159).**

TRAVEL STRESS

160 **Leave a paper trail.** Before embarking on your travels, leave photocopies of your passport, tickets, insurance details and travel cheques with family or friends. If your documents get lost or stolen, you will be able to get at the necessary information with minimum disruption to your trip.

161 **Go to bed at the local time** when you arrive at your destination. During long-haul flights it is common to cross several time-zones in a short space of time. Time differences, combined with cramped and dehydrating conditions on the flight, can lead to symptoms of jet lag upon arrival. These

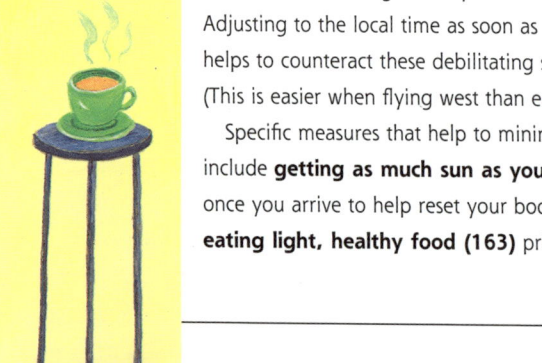

include extreme fatigue and poor concentration. Adjusting to the local time as soon as possible helps to counteract these debilitating symptoms. (This is easier when flying west than east.)

Specific measures that help to minimize jet lag include **getting as much sun as you can (162)** once you arrive to help reset your body clock; **eating light, healthy food (163)** prior to and

during travel to place minimal stress on the digestive system; **drinking plenty of water (164)** and **avoiding tea, coffee, alcohol and caffeinated fizzy drinks (165)** (which have diuretic effects) prior to and during the flight to minimize dehydration; **getting up and walking around (166)** on the plane.

167 **Perform leg exercises** during flights to ward off DVT (deep vein thrombosis). DVT occurs when a (potentially fatal) blood clot forms in the body. During the enforced inertia of flights, leg exercises help to encourage the free flow of blood through the limbs. Every half an hour, rotate and flex your ankles and squeeze your leg muscles twenty times. Every hour or so, get up from your seat and stretch your legs.

168 **Banish boredom** by refusing to fight it. Treat the time you have at your disposal as a luxury – a welcome opportunity to exercise your imagination.

169 **Be a hero of time.** If you are delayed during your journey, think of waiting as a challenge to your inner strength – but one that you can vanquish without difficulty. As you sit or stand there, feel yourself growing in stature with every minute that you wait. Enjoy the quality of time as it passes: see it as an invisible heroic frieze that celebrates your conquest of boredom.

170 Pause once you get into your car. Before fastening your seat belt, putting your key in the ignition or adjusting your mirrors, take a few moments to think about some of the people you love. Make a commitment to yourself, your family and other loved ones to drive calmly and safely today.

171 Relax your hands while driving: see how lightly you can hold the wheel while continuing to steer. If you are gripping the wheel, it can be a sign that you are tense or frustrated – perhaps with slow traffic or other drivers. If this is the case you may be holding tension in other parts of your body as well.

Rotate your hands (172) to free your wrists when stuck in traffic: lift one hand off the steering wheel and gently make circles with the hand, rotating in both directions. Return your hand to the wheel before repeating the action with the other hand.

Perform shoulder rolls (173) at traffic lights, moving your shoulders up, back, down and around in a continuous movement to reduce neck and shoulder tension. Repeat ten times. **Practise chin tucks (174)** while driving. Looking straight ahead, tuck in your chin (pretend that you're trying to give yourself a double chin while moving your head back toward the head rest). This exercise will help to lessen neck strain and prevent you from slouching forward.

175 **Reconsider your attitude** toward other drivers. Are you impatient, pressing right up behind other drivers to pressure them to go faster? Are you overly competitive, overtaking other cars for the sake of it? If so, take a deep breath and focus your attention on the purpose of your journey – namely, reaching your destination without endangering yourself or others.

To encourage yourself to remain calm, **drive more slowly (176)**: find a quiet spot in the slow lane and simply coast along. At the same time, **play an affirmation tape (177)** to focus your mind, or some **soft jazz (178)** to soothe your nerves.

Positive change

179 **Run through the ABCD of change:** A is for Awareness of what you need to change. B is for Belief in your ability to change. C is for Commitment to the idea of change. D is for Discipline and your willingness to stick to your plan of change.

180 **Reawaken your choices.** We tend to forget that we have choices at many levels. We can choose the direction of our lives, the thoughts and reactions that we have, even the feelings we create. Cultivating awareness of how we are creating our current experiences – of what we're doing and why we're doing it – gives us the freedom to create different experiences by making alternative choices.

181 **See life as a journey,** not a destination. Destination consciousness (a constant preoccupation with future goals) ensnares us in anxieties related to time as we fret about our progress. By contrast, journey consciousness (an openness to the present moment) enables us to appreciate the delights and lessons that greet us at every twist and turn along the way.

182 **Enjoy your own freshness.** Life takes place in the present moment; past and future exist only in your imagination. Relish the experience of living in the now – the sensations that feed your senses, the currents of energy that percolate your being.

183 **Create a positive self-image** on the screen of your mind. Visualize yourself as the most positive human being that ever existed. Compose a complete profile of this super-positive person – including their facial expressions, the clothes they're

wearing, how they're feeling. Now step into the screen image and start to inhabit it. See life through the eyes of this super-positive person – these are your eyes now and this is your life.

184   **Find the silver lining** in every cloud. Whatever adversity you face, always look for the spark of hope, the positive angle, the hidden benefit. Visualize this as a beam of light piercing the darkness inside your heart and reinforcing your belief in yourself and your abilities to move forward to brighter times ahead.

185   **Ban self-denying phrases,** such as "I can't" or "I don't do things like that," from your vocabulary: they tend to become self-fulfilling prophecies by their very utterance.

Similarly, **ban habitual expressions of procrastination (186),** such as "I'll start tomorrow," and **phrases of displaced initiative (187)** such as "Is there a plan?" Our choice of words tends to reflect our thinking. If we are able to change what we say after becoming aware of the phrases we use, it becomes possible to change what we think and ultimately what we do.

188 **Collect 100 affirmations** (see point 51, page 32) for
coping with a variety of problems and events. Write each of
them into a letter-indexed address book, under the situation it
relates to. For example, record "I am a talented, enthusiastic
and committed worker" under the heading Job Interview; or
"My wisdom and beauty increase with age" under Birthdays.
Use these affirmations as and when the occasion arises.

189 **Act "as if."** Our minds are very suggestible. If you act as if
you are serene, happy and free of stress, eventually you may
find that it becomes a reality.

190 **Remember there are no mistakes,** only opportunities for
learning, growth and change.

191 **Switch on the light.** Feeling down without knowing why is
a common experience. In such moments we may let out a silent
cry for help – forgetting sometimes that we can help ourselves.
If you find yourself in this position, imagine that you are in a

dark room. The room is your life and the darkness your mood of gloom. Now reach out and switch on the light. Amazingly the room is filled with reasons to be cheerful. On a pad of paper, write or draw everything that you see. Carry this record around with you to provide yourself with a ready source of inspiration.

Alternatively, you may prefer to **carry symbols (192)** of your reasons to be cheerful around with you – perhaps a photograph of a loved one in a locket or wallet, or a glorious flower worn in a buttonhole to remind you of the beauties of nature.

193 **Appreciate last year's gifts.** Although New Year's resolutions are useful for setting the course for the following year, they can imply flaws and failings in the past. For a truly positive start to the new year it's important to find value in the one that's just ended. Reflect on the experiences that you found most challenging and think of three positive outcomes for each one that you can carry forward into the next year – perhaps lessons you have learned, wonderful people you have met, inner strengths you have discovered.

194 **Match your values and goals** in order to feel fulfilled in what you do. If there's a gap between the two, you will experience either tension or apathy. High values plus empty goals equals no motivation to reach your targets. Low values plus ambitious goals equals no real satisfaction in your achievements. Ask yourself which are more positive: your values or your goals? Make any necessary adjustments to either in order to bring the two factors into line with each other, thereby correcting any inner disharmony.

195 **Look at the big and small.** Think about the subjects to which you pay most attention: which of them have become too dominant in your life? Now consider areas you may be neglecting. Awareness of imbalances of this kind often provides sufficient motivation to effect a redistribution of energies.

   Repeat this process using images (196) to effect a mental shift at a deeper level. In the foreground of your mental landscape, visualize an object to represent the area of your life that has become too dominant; in the background visualize an

object to represent the area that has been neglected. Now
see if you can mentally change your position so that you view
the objects from the other side. The foreground object now
becomes the background object and vice versa.

197   **Surround yourself with positive images.** Much of the
information we receive and entertainment we watch is laced
with negative energy. Over time this negativity has a subtle yet
damaging effect on our perceptions and feelings. To counter
this, surround yourself with images that are life-affirming,
optimistic or inspirational: for example, you could fill your
home with fresh flowers, go for walks in a park or the
countryside, even plant some trees in your neighbourhood.

Similarly, **fill your ears with positive sounds (198)** – listen
to birdsong, play upbeat music, install a fountain in the garden.
Where possible it is also important to **filter out negative
stimuli (199)**. For example, clear your living and working
environments of dirt and disorder; pick up litter when you're out
and about; refuse to listen to malicious gossip; carefully select

what you see and hear in the media, limiting your exposure to war and violence to the level that is necessary for an awareness of what is happening in the world.

200   Wear an exotic or unusual hat – unusual for you, that is! However out of character it seems, it is unlikely that people will judge or challenge you – they will probably admire your courage. You could be teased by close friends and family, or by your partner, but they'll soon get used to the new, more adventurous you. It's a good way to prove to yourself that nothing about your habits is absolutely fixed: change is always possible.

Alternatively, make a similar statement in a minor key with a pair of outrageous red **shoes (201)** or some wacky **sunglasses (202)**.

203   **Vote for yourself** every morning, as if you are the leader for the party of Everlasting Happiness, and every day is election day! Imagine what you would promise in your victory speech. Polish your speech a little more each day. See yourself walking your talk.

204   **Chart your daily moods** in your diary – perhaps by using some kind of coding system. If you are prone to mood swings, you might find it helpful to do this either hour by hour or for every morning, afternoon and evening. Using the information gleaned from this exercise, you should be able to replicate the beneficial circumstances more often, and avoid any stressors until you become strong enough to remain unaffected by them.

205 **Do more of what you're good at.** It's almost certain to be something you enjoy and, as a bonus, this will strengthen your self-confidence.

206 **Try something new** at least once a month – whether it's reading a classic children's book, joining a tango class, or riding pillion on a motorbike. Exposing yourself to unfamiliar experiences stretches your mental and physical horizons, acclimatizing you to change and loosening the grip of routine.

207 **Admit when you don't know.** In today's world we are constantly pressurized to have answers to and opinions about everything. Such pressures may make us painfully conscious of the gaps in our knowledge, whether in politics, economics, history, the arts or any other field. However, there is no need to feel guilty about what you don't know. Refuse to join the ranks of those who claim to be an instant expert on topics of popular interest. Nobody can know something about everything. Accept your blind spots, and don't be stressed about them.

208 **Admit you were wrong** when you know, deep down, that you were. This instantly frees you from the tension created by sustaining the illusion that you were right!

209 **Give up on your book** if you're not enjoying it. Find one that does please you. You owe no obligation to any writer.

210 **Try to eliminate your tics of speech** – for example, repeatedly saying "you know." Strive to express yourself more precisely. In doing so you will communicate more effectively, and discover a new source of self-esteem.

211 **Give up an addictive substance** such as tobacco, sugar or alcohol. Not only should you find that your health improves, but freedom from dependency will give you a greater sense of empowerment.

Overcome undesirable habits (212), such as unpunctuality. Whenever you are late for something, ask yourself what was more important to you than being on time. If you didn't leave enough time to reach your destination, then you may have valued your comfort more than your commitment. Do not judge your response. Simply use it as information about your hidden motivations. Once aware of your motives, you can make more informed choices in future.

213   **Find an amulet** – smooth objects, such as buttons, coins or stones, are ideal. Carry it with you, rubbing it with your fingers to reinforce the promises that you make to yourself. Amulets with **personal significance (214)** are often the most potent.

TIME AND MONEY

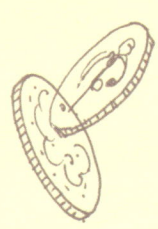

215   **Depose King Time.** Fighting against the relentless onward march of time is a common source of anxiety. At weekends, and during time off work, remove your watch to give you some respite from time's tyranny.

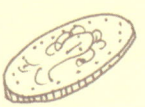

216   **Treat time as a convenience,** not an obstacle. Time is merely nature's way of preventing everything from happening at once. Think of it as a robotic helper, programmed to remain in the background until it's required – for example, when you are meeting a friend in a restaurant.

217   **Do less, experience more.** In our fast-paced modern world, there is a constant pressure to do more in less time. Consequently, there is little time to appreciate what we are doing, to enjoy the experience of being alive.

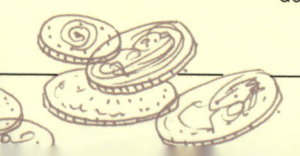

One way to ease this situation is to schedule in some time for yourself. To do this you may need to reduce the number of commitments you take on. With less to do you will have more time to reflect on and appreciate your experiences.

Consider down-sizing (218). A more drastic step, for those who are comfortable in money but poor in time, is to work shorter hours for less pay. This could involve a shift from full-time to part-time employment, taking a step down the career ladder, or even a complete change in career. Think seriously about it: many people find it immeasurably enriching.

219 **Pay bills on time** to keep your creditors happy and avoid late payment charges. Keep a large envelope in a convenient place and pop bills into it as they arrive. Deal with the contents at a set time each week so that it becomes second nature to you.

220 **Save, save, save.** Do the arithmetic to work out how you can make savings throughout the year. If you have to cut out certain luxuries, think of them as attachments you are letting go of.

221 **Have an expense-free day** – with a little forward planning this should be possible, even on a work day (for example, you may need to prepare a packed lunch to take into the office). See how many you can have in a week. It's a great way of saving.

222 **Be mindful of money** – in other words, ask yourself what money means to you. Try to concentrate on its practical rather than its symbolic value. Don't allow a connection to take root between money and self-esteem. Your true assets are your personal values, not your monetary valuation. Even when money is elusive, you have the power to thrive, as a loving, peaceful being.

223 **Create a money magnet.** Whenever small change clutters up your purse or wallet, empty it into a jar. Over time the money will accumulate until you have a significant amount. Change the coins for notes at a bank and spend the money on a treat for yourself, or donate it to a charitable cause.

LONG-TERM CHANGES

224 Make a life-plan. Write a list of ten things that you want to happen in your life, from places you want to visit to events you want to bring about. Tick them off as you achieve them. With each tick you'll feel a sense of fulfilling your own destiny.

225 Snapshot your goals. One reason that many of us lack concrete goals is that we don't have a clear picture of them. Imagine that your mind is a camera. Now create detailed mental images of your goals in your life's key areas – career, family, relationships, personal growth. One by one press the button to open the shutter and imprint your goals on your mind.

Go out and take actual photographs (226) of subjects that represent your goals. Display the photos in your bedroom, study or kitchen to inspire you to move forward.

227 Look where you're going – rather than focusing on the obstacles that lie in your way. The obstacles may be imaginary, but even if they're real, you won't get far if you allow them to dominate your whole field of vision.

228 **Write a mission statement** on a page of your diary – preferably at the beginning of each year. In two or three sentences, the statement should summarize your main aims for the year as specifically as possible. Clearly defining your purpose in this way will give you direction and focus your energies.

Once every three months you may wish to **reassess (229)** your mission statement, modifying it to reflect your thinking as it changes. We are all entitled to develop in unexpected directions – that's part of the satisfaction of being human.

Alongside your mission statement, **write a guarantee (230)** specifying the ways in which you vow to behave in order to achieve your goals for the year.

231 **Make a motor of change.** Assemble a patchwork of inspiring words and images. Leaf through old magazines, cutting out any passages or pictures that represent your goals or aspirations. Stick them onto a sheet of cardboard to form a collage. Pin this to your kitchen noticeboard as an encouragement to take steps toward your dreams.

232   **Plan a strategy of change**. Although change is exciting
and stimulating, with the potential to expand our horizons, it
can also be painful and scary, forcing us to abandon our
comfort zones. Forming a plan will help you to embrace change,
because it will outline the steps you need to take in order to
reach your goals, and in the process it will reveal those steps as
perfectly realistic. Not only will your strategy make your goals
seem more achievable, it will also give you a structure with
which to stabilize yourself as you step out into the unknown.

233   **Take baby steps.** Often the best way to progress toward
a goal is to take one small action each day that brings your
dreams closer to fruition. For example, you might spend a
lunchtime gathering information on the internet, write an
email requesting a brochure, or make a phone call to
someone who can help you.

234   **Find a role model.** Look for someone who has achieved the
kind of goals that you are aiming for. See what you can find out

about the steps they took and the strategies they used to arrive at their current position. Perhaps you could write to them or give them a phone call asking for their advice. Alternatively, if they are in the public eye, you might come across informative interviews with them or books about their lives.

235 **Find a dream-buddy.** Following your dreams can be scary, so it can be useful to find someone who will support you on your chosen path. An ideal dream-buddy might be a positive and supportive friend who is likewise contemplating change. Make a commitment to call one another each week to report on the progress you have made and offer each other encouragement.

236 **Never stop learning** – about yourself, other people, and the world at large. Learning ensures that we remain flexible and responsive, able to deal with whatever happens to us and make the changes that we seek.

237   **Learn a new skill.** Whether completely different from your other activities, or complementary to them, a new skill will expand your potential, thereby benefiting all areas of your life.

238   **Speak of what you're doing,** not what you're *trying* to do. To "try" admits the possibility of failure. In telling yourself that you are already doing something (not merely trying), you are helping to bring about a self-fulfilling expectation of success.

239   **Don't try to turn chalk to cheese,** or vice versa. Your attitudes can be transformed, but only in gentle steps. If you're an extrovert, by all means aim to listen more, or show off less, but don't seek to become an introvert. Likewise, if you are an introvert, by all means try to be more open with people, or go to more parties, but don't try to become an extrovert. The key is to find your strengths and work within them.

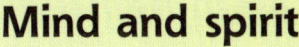

Mind and spirit

240 **Develop your meditation posture.** In order to relax during meditation it is important to sit comfortably. The traditional position for practising meditation is the lotus posture (sitting with both legs crossed, the tops of the feet resting on the opposite thighs). **Easier versions (241)** are the half-lotus (sitting, one foot resting on the opposite thigh), or simply sitting upright on the floor with the legs crossed. If you feel any pain in your knees in these positions, place a cushion under your pelvis.

Alternatively, **sit on an upright chair (242)** with your legs uncrossed. Sit forward on the seat so that your back isn't resting on the back of the chair.

243 **Meditate regularly** – at least once a week, preferably daily. Although the ideal time to practise meditation is in the morning (see points 15 and 16, page

21), you can meditate anywhere and at any time. To encourage you to practise regularly, find a time that suits your daily schedule. Initially, choose a quiet part of the day, when you will be free from other demands on your attention.

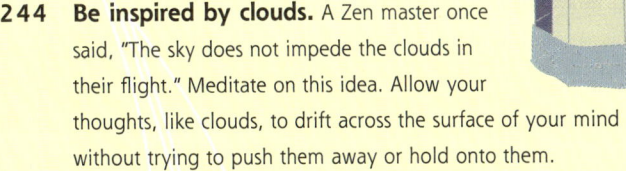

244   Be inspired by clouds. A Zen master once said, "The sky does not impede the clouds in their flight." Meditate on this idea. Allow your thoughts, like clouds, to drift across the surface of your mind without trying to push them away or hold onto them.

245   Meditate on a candle. Place a lighted candle before you in your meditation space. Focus your gaze on the flame of the candle until you can see nothing but light bordered by shadows. Lower your eyelids slowly until your eyes are almost closed. You will see shafts of golden light shooting out from the flame. Imagine that these are sparks of spirit – a quiver of vitality at the core of your being. (Follow safety precautions: see page 207.)

246 **Meditate light-heartedly.** If you find it hard to relax and free your thoughts during meditation, it may be because you are tense or anxious. Before you start your session, think of something funny – humour is profoundly liberating to the spirit.

247 **Meditate on a mandala.** Mandalas are concentric geometrical patterns representing the cosmos (see picture, left). They are used in Hindu and Buddhist traditions as aids to meditation. The idea is to focus on the patterns of the mandala in order to achieve a profound sense of oneness with the universe. Start by contemplating the centre, then move outward, allowing the forms to fill your mind. Let the harmony of the mandala resonate deep within you.

248 **Meditate on the yin-yang symbol.** This is a Taoist emblem (right) whose rotational symmetry suggests a dynamic interplay between two polar yet complementary opposites. Use this idea of the harmony of opposites as the basis for meditations on a relationship where there is conflict between you.

249 **Meditate on your hands.** Clench your fists with your knuckles upward as if grasping a pencil. Now let go: the pencil drops and you have lost it. Now grasp the imaginary pencil with your knuckles face down. Release your grasp: this time the pencil remains in your hand. Letting go need not mean loss. An open hand represents relaxation, a grasping hand represents tension and stress. As you meditate see if you can open your mind in the same way. Pay attention to any shifts that occur. Is there a sense of release? A loosening of your grip on fixed ways of perceiving and responding to the world?

250   Meditate on the face of your watch. (Ideally it should have a second hand.) As you gaze at your watch, fill your consciousness with nothing but the circle of the face. As you do so you will notice that the second hand seems to come to a stop. It is as if you have entered a realm that is free from the constraints of time and space – the ultimate relaxation.

251   Meditate on the pattern of a leaf. First get a sense of the overall pattern by scanning its main features. Do not attempt to find meaning in the pattern, simply allow the

shapes, lines and colours to penetrate your unconscious, aware
that the image is both in front of you and inside your mind.

Using the same technique, contemplate **a flower (252)**,
ideally a fragrant one that remains attached to the plant. Focus

on the shape, colour and texture of the petals. Close your eyes and smell the perfume. Drinking in the essence of a flower in this way is as refreshing and nourishing as a herbal drink.

Composite flowers (253), such as gerberas and chrysanthemums, have many petals, all arranged into concentric patterns that provide natural mandalas for meditation.

In fact, you can treat any pattern, natural or man-made, as the focus for meditation. For example, a **decorative plate (254)**, a **motif in a piece of fabric (255)**, even the **creases in the palm of your hand (256)**.

257   Muse on a paradox. The Greek philosopher, Empedocles, once said: "God is a circle whose centre is everywhere and whose circumference is nowhere." Such conundrums defy rational understanding, hinting at truths deeper than words can express. To appreciate their meaning we must allow them to hang in our minds without seeking logical explanations.

Treat **koans (258)** (paradoxical stories from the Zen tradition) in the same way, dwelling on them in meditation.

259 **The empty vessel meditation** is designed to heighten your awareness of the relationship between space and form. Visualize an empty tea cup. Both its form and the space it contains within itself are crucial to its function as a carrier for liquid. As you hold the teacup in your mind, keep these two elements in balance with each other.

260 **Meditate on a Chinese dragon.** An emblem of the Emperor, the Chinese dragon is a potent symbol combining strength, perseverance, courage and excellence. Whenever you face obstacles, find the dragon within yourself, and draw on its energies to overcome them.

261   **Contemplate duality.** Taking a coin, look first at the side bearing a head. As if seeing through the head, visualize an image of the obverse side of the coin. Then turn the coin and do the same with the other side. In the two-sided coin we find a symbol of duality, a reminder of the multi-faceted nature of reality. There is always more than one way of looking at things.

262   **Meditate on extremophiles** to refresh your wonder at the miraculous resilience of life. Extremophiles are microscopic creatures able to survive in extreme conditions, such as the core of a volcano. The human spirit is similarly indestructible. Locate the invincible spirit within yourself: feel it inhabiting every corner of your inner realm.

263   **Drill to the core** in your meditations, as though drilling for oil. You will need patience as you work through different layers of your psyche to reach the core of consciousness. Imagine the drill-head of your focused attention slicing through your accumulated layers of experiences, memories, perceptions, beliefs, until finally you break through to pure love, pure peace, pure contentment at the centre of your being.

264 **Use a mantra** in your meditation. A mantra is a word or sound that is repeated over and over again to provide a focus for the mind during meditation. Perhaps the best-known mantra is "Om". According to Hindu belief, Om is the primordial sound from which the entire universe was created. Chanting this syllable is believed to bring the chanter in harmony with the energies of the cosmos. When chanting Om, sound the final consonant for about four seconds, so that it becomes a hum.

You could also **chant an appropriate word (265)**, such as "calm", where again you can linger on the final m.

266 **Dissolve your body** in a visualization. Lie comfortably on your back. Starting at the toes and working toward your head, imagine your body turning to liquid as you tense, then relax, each part in turn. Finish by relaxing the mind, concentrating deeply, then letting your thoughts dissolve and float away.

267 **Visualize little balls of light** in a box. In your mind, open the box and take out the balls, placing each in turn on an area of your body that is tight or tense. Imagine the light dissolving into your body, relaxing and healing as it does so.

268 **Visualize a lotus floating on a pond.** Imagine light pouring outward through the petals, filling you with radiance. The lotus is a symbol for the spirit. As you practise this meditation, feel the deep calm that spiritual radiance brings.

269   Take leave of your senses. This meditation involves
concentrating on the core of your self while remaining aware
of sensual experience on the periphery. Sitting in your chosen
meditation posture, close your eyes. In your mind, check off
what you see, hear, feel, smell, taste. Revisiting each sensation
in turn, say goodbye to each of them. As you do so, dedicate
the portion of attention that was absorbed in your senses to
your spirit, at the core of your being. Remain in this state of
spiritual freedom for as long as you can.

270 **Visualize your star,** a point of light in the centre of your forehead, just above your eyes. According to some Eastern traditions this is the "third eye" and represents the seat of intuition. Feel your star radiating energy. Whenever you require strength or inspiration, call it to mind and allow it to guide you.

271 **Visualize the sun's journey through the day,** starting with a glimmering dawn, passing noon, then ending in a glorious sunset. An apt metaphor for human life, this image serves as a reminder of the beauty and value of all stages of life, and of the eternal cycle of renewal.

272 **Visualize a golden gate** to summon up a sense of strength and protection. Imagine the gate in as much detail as possible. It could be the entrance to a Chinese imperial palace,

or a hidden gate to a beautiful wild garden: let your mood inform your choice. Simply absorb the image into your mind and allow its subtle influence to work on your unconscious.

You can combine any symbol and colour in this way to fortify yourself with a particular quality, summoned from your inner depth by meditation. Let your imagination develop appropriate symbolism. For example, expansive **green fields and lawns (273)** evoke a sense of balance and harmony. If these qualities suggest contact with others, you might choose to populate the scene with loved ones. Or if you're inclined toward solitude, trees and animals might provide the only company.

A bowl of oranges (274) suggests energy and radiance. Concentrate not only on the fruit but also on the setting and the design on the bowl. A handful of **red-brown earth (275)** is

associated with stability and continuity. Consider the origin of this earth – perhaps it comes from a place that has a particularly grounding influence upon you? A **red rose (276)** symbolizes unconditional love. Perhaps the rose is being offered as a token, or is blooming in a garden? A **deep blue lake (277)** evokes profound serenity. Is it surrounded by lowland, or hilly or mountainous countryside? What creatures are swimming in the lake? A **blue sky (278)** evokes freedom and expansion. If there are clouds, decide whether they are puffs of white or an ominous gray. The images that we create for ourselves are the most powerful, so use these examples as starting-points for creating your own personalized collection of symbols and hues.

279 **Imagine yourself diving into the sea.** The moment your body penetrates the surface, the water transforms into light. Gently, weightlessly, you glide through the brightness. You come to a halt, poised within the luminescence that embraces you. You are aware of tremendous power. Absorb this power: it gives you everything you will ever need.

280 **Imagine yourself as seaweed** rooted to the seabed and moving back and forth with the current. Sway with the rhythm of the water, in perfect harmony with your surroundings.

281 **Think of yourself as a tree,** flourishing and growing in all weathers and conditions; your wounds, the knots and twisted branches bearing testament to life's struggles. It is in these seeming imperfections that true beauty lies – the source of your uniqueness and strength.

282 **Visualize a wind** blowing straight through you as you stand against it. As it whistles through your body, imagine it unpicking the threads of every negative thought and feeling that has ever been woven into the fabric of your being.

283 **Become the sky.** Visualize the vast blue sky above. Be aware that it is without limits, without boundaries, embracing the world. Consider that our minds, and therefore our whole selves too, are without limits or boundaries. As the sky fills your mind, experience the boundlessness of self and spirit – infinitely rich, infinitely calm. Do not strain to capture infinity – just relax in acceptance of the boundless sky inside and outside your boundless consciousness.

284 **Visualize a sunrise across a mountain lake.** As the sun peeps above the horizon, the first shafts of light stream across the dark water toward you, bathing your face in their warm caress. It is your spiritual dawn. The rays of the sun have

brought you the two most precious gifts of the spirit – the
light of truth and awareness, and the warmth of love and
compassion. Allow your heart and mind to be kissed by the
sun. Feel the glow penetrate to the very depths of your being.

285 **Play to an empty theatre.** Imagine you are walking into
the auditorium of a huge theatre just as the audience is leaving
after a performance. The stage is being cleared. You wander
onto the now empty stage and sit on a chair looking out across
the endless rows of vacant seats. You are struck by the absolute
stillness. Your mind becomes empty like the stage. Your heart
becomes silent like the auditorium. Your spirit is at peace.

286 **Find the tower of wisdom.** Imagine arriving in a remote
village in the Himalayas. The focal point of the village is a
square tower dedicated to an ancient Buddhist monk. The
tower is decorated with four faces: peace, love, truth and
happiness – one on each side. Wander slowly around the tower,
pausing to meditate on each face in turn. Allow the faces to

speak to you, permeating your spirit with their profound and reassuring messages.

287   Send a message in a bottle. There are times when we feel like emotional castaways, lost and alone, stranded on the island of our sorrows. Whenever you feel this way, visualize yourself writing out your worries on a sheet of paper. In your mind roll it up tight and insert it into a bottle. Throw the bottle out into the ocean. Watch it bob upon the waves until it disappears from sight. Picture someone finding the bottle and reading your message. Contact has been made. You are no longer alone.

288 **Turn water into light.** Sit quietly in your meditation space, eyes closed, attending only to your breath. You sense a mysterious figure approach you carrying an urn filled with water. With a cupped hand, they lift some water from the urn and pour it over your head. As the water splashes onto your head it transforms into light, suffusing you with peace and renewed energy.

289 **Air-lift your garbage.** Imagine waking up one morning to the whirring sound of helicopters overhead. To a rope dropped by the first helicopter you attach a box containing all your negative thoughts. Up and away it flies. The second helicopter removes your worries, the third, your emotional baggage. Half an hour and ten helicopters later you feel lighter, fully relieved of your unwanted detritus.

SPIRITUALITY

290   **Develop a spiritual practice.** Any activity that serves to centre you, bringing you a sense of deep inner connection with both
yourself and the world around you, can form the basis for a spiritual practice. Examples include Eastern disciplines, such as yoga
and meditation, as well as various aspects of Buddhism and Zen,
such as the spiritual pilgrimage and the tea ceremony (see points
408, page 179; and 448, page 192). The activity will absorb you
completely, so that you reach a state of "flow" whereby you are
one with what you are doing. Practise this as regularly as
possible – it will give you a point of steadiness in your life.

291   **Learn from spiritual
teachers,** such as the Buddha
or St Augustine. Study their
lives and teachings and follow
their precepts in small but
important ways. Ask yourself
whether they would approve of
actions you are contemplating.

292 **Be humble.** As Henry Thoreau once said, "Humility like darkness reveals the heavenly lights."

293 **Cradle yourself** in the hand of Destiny. Picture a softly lit room, its walls covered in soft fabrics, and in the middle of the room an enormous upturned hand. Climb into the hand and curl up in its cushioned palm. Feel the fingers gently close around you, enveloping you in protection and love. You are resting in the hand of Destiny.

294 **Meet your angel.** Close your eyes and imagine yourself at the edge of a dark forest. Ahead of you is a path. You follow the path, which winds deep into the heart of the forest. Eventually you come to a clearing where there is a temple. A bright white light is emanating from the doorway. As you enter the temple, you see that the brightness is in fact a beautiful angel – a being of light. The angel holds out its arms and you embrace. In that moment of connection you realize that your angel knows and understands everything about you and your

life. It is your companion on your journey and will always be there for you to offer unconditional love and support. Whenever you feel lost or alone, simply return to this sacred place within yourself and your angel will be there to greet you.

295 **Call on your spirit guides.** Whether you understand them as the embodiment of your inner spiritual wisdom, or as all-knowing celestial beings akin to guardian angels, your spirit guides can be of help whenever you are faced with a difficult situation, or have a question that you are unable to answer. Just think, speak or write your question. You will receive the answer through one of a number of different routes – for example, in a dream, during a conversation with someone, or in a book that you are given, recommended or impelled to buy. Simply pay heed to the signs all around you.

296 **Follow the Tao.** *Tao* is a Chinese word, meaning "the way" or "the path". Taoism is an Eastern philosophy based on the principle that life involves a ceaseless movement and flow from one form to another. Problems arise when we attempt to resist or control the natural pattern of change. Harmony can be restored by following the Tao – that is, by "going with the flow", accepting the ever-changing pattern of life without judgment or resistance.

297 **See dying as a gift** and you will no longer live in fear of death. As the American poet Emily Dickinson put it: "Dying is a wild night and a new road." If we thought we were going to live forever, we would feel terribly trapped in our lives.

Alternatively, think of death as a **homecoming (298)** – the point where the river reaches the sea, where the soul is reunited with its source.

299 **Visit a graveyard.** The peaceful atmosphere of most grave-yards makes them ideal places for quiet reflection. Read the epitaphs. Feel a sense of oneness with life's eternal rhythms.

300 **Create a personal altar** in a quiet corner of your home – ideally in a private room, such as a bedroom or study. Cover a small table or box with a cloth and decorate it with items that represent your sources of inspiration and strength. These could include photographs of family and friends, flowers and stones symbolizing the natural world, and so on. Meditate or pray in front of your altar. Feel its beneficial energies.

301 **Buy a statuette** or icon that represents the values you believe in and display it prominently to remind you of your ideals. The spiritually minded might opt for a religious figure, such as the Buddha, whose Truth (*dharma*) is designed to appeal to everyone, regardless of rank or class, inviting us to follow the path to enlightenment and the cessation of suffering. Other spiritual figures include the many-armed Hindu god Shiva and the Taoist Immortals.

Alternatively, display some imperishable **natural form (302)**, such as a seashell or a pine cone, as a symbol of your love for the world.

303 **Discover the power of prayer.** Everyone can benefit from prayer, whether religious or not. In prayer we express our hopes and dreams, as well as acknowledging our blessings. In so doing we both affirm our direction in life, and draw upon the strengths that we need to continue our journey. Your prayer can take whatever form you choose. Address it to your source of wisdom and strength: this could be your higher self, the universe, or the divine as you understand it.

304 **Drop a coin in a wishing well** or fountain and make a wish for good things to happen to a friend, or even an enemy, as you throw the coin into the water. A benevolent heart is always more content than one that is merely concerned with itself.

305 **Make a wishing tree.** Wishing trees originate from a Celtic tradition which involves tying coloured scraps of clothing, called "clouties", to a tree and making a wish. To make your own wishing tree, find an old item of clothing that you are ready to part with. After ripping the clothing into shreds, find a suitable tree and tie one of the pieces of cloth onto it, making a wish or creating a goal as you do so. Repeat this until your tree is hung

with all your life goals. Through this ritual you release the weight of the past and allow your vision to invoke your future.

306 **Use a balloon** as a messenger for your wishes. Having formulated a wish, write it on a piece of paper and tie it to a helium-filled balloon. Take the balloon outside and release it to the skies. Watch the balloon diminish to a vivid speck as it carries your wish out into the ether. Taking positive action in this way will encourage you to work toward realizing your desire and perhaps prompt destiny to respond by supporting you.

As your thoughts create a reality, performing this action **in your imagination (307)** can be equally powerful, provided that you take time to envisage all the steps in detail.

308 **Purge your fears** with a ritual burning. Write them on a piece of paper, and either throw the paper into the flames of a fire, or light it with a candle and dispose of it safely. Make this affirmation: "My fear is within my control. I banish it to oblivion."

309 **Reconnect with the elements.** Whenever you find yourself distracted or agitated, unable to remain present in a given situation, use the elements to ground yourself and regain a natural perspective. For example, you could walk barefoot outside; sit or lie on the ground; let sand or pebbles run through your fingers; surround yourself with candles; swim or float in a lake; even lean into a high wind, allowing the air to support you.

If it's inconvenient to perform any of these activities, practise the **elements meditation (310)** instead. According to Eastern traditions, the entire physical universe is made up of the five elements – fire, water, air, earth and ether. Meditate on the unique qualities of each of these elements; and end with a prayer of thanks for firemen, sailors, pilots and miners who grapple with the four main elements for our benefit.

311 **Lie on the ground and gaze at the sky.** From this perspective we can appreciate the true vastness of the sky as it arches above us, holding both the Earth and ourselves in its supportive embrace. We become more deeply aware of our intrinsic connection with the cosmos, the small but vital role we play in the order of nature.

Watch clouds (312) floating by. Allow your mind to free-associate – what do the shapes call to mind? Can you see any familiar people or objects? Reflect on what you see. Take time out from your routine and live among the clouds for a while.

313 Watch a plane fly by. Rather than viewing this as a source of noise pollution, acknowledge the miracle of flight. See if you can intuit the plane's destination. Conjure up that place in your mind. Imagine the passengers sitting in the plane. Wish them *bon voyage.*

314 A double rainbow is an extraordinary phenomenon. See it as a reminder of the uniqueness of your life and a blessing on all you do. Relish the experience and be thankful for the privilege of this auspicious signal from nature.

Of all must-see natural phenomena, top of the league is the **aurora borealis (315)**, the northern lights, a shimmering curtain of light that will send tingles down your spine. The equivalent in the southern hemisphere is the aurora australis.

316   **Listen to the rain.** The insistent rhythm of raindrops bouncing off a roof or onto a backyard can have a lulling effect. During the day, appreciate the rain's ability to block out less welcome sounds; at night, relish the snugness of being warm and dry in bed as the rain falls.

317   **Walk in the rain** without an umbrella when it's warm outside. Take pleasure in the water droplets as they hit your body, trickling in cool rivulets over your skin. Enjoy the feeling of intimacy

with the elements – it is a reminder of our connection with
the natural world.

318 **Hug a tree.** Aficionados of the mind-body-spirit movement are
often nicknamed "tree-huggers": why not live up to the name?
Many cultures believe that trees have healing properties and can
dispel negative energy from a person without harm to the tree.

Choose **oak (319)** for luck and strength; **ash (320)** for peace
and prosperity; **maple (321)** for longevity and love; and **willow
(322)** for protection and energy.

323 **Sit at the base of a pine tree** and meditate on its
symbolic associations with wisdom, maturity and longevity.

324 **Float in a pool, lake or sea.** Stretch out your arms and
legs, surrendering all attempts to control your movement. Just
lie there, enjoying both weightlessness and "will-lessness".
Imagine all your roles in life, and all your worries, rising off
you like steam. You are pure self, pure mind, pure spirit.

ACCEPTANCE

325 **Trust in life's flow.** If you find that you are struggling to achieve a desired result in any situation, it could be that you are trying to force the issue. Instead, sit back and accept whatever happens. That which is rightly yours will come to you. Nothing takes place before its designated time.

326 **Accept change.** Nothing stays the same forever. True relaxation comes not from controlling life's flow, but from allowing yourself to be carried along by the flow without fear of the future or nostalgia for the past.

327 **Meditate on bird migration** in order to reconcile yourself to change. Year in, year out, birds experience the seasonal upheavals of migration. However, these global movements are not seen as disruptive: they are simply a manifestation of the ebb and

flow of nature's cycles. In the same way,
understand the changes in your life as part
of a broader pattern of cyclical change
instead of obstacles on a linear trail.

328   Visualize a week-old sparrow
holding tight onto a branch. Its first flight is just moments away.
The chick looks up as its mother glides past, inviting it to take to
the air. In accord with its natural impulses, the chick lets go of
the branch. Down toward the earth it plunges at first, until
suddenly, flapping its wings, it recovers, finding the strength
and skill to rise and soar. The bird gives a heartfelt squawk
of gleeful achievement – its rite of passage successfully
completed. Hidden within this visualization is a simple message:
let go of your branch. Detachment brings freedom, which in
turn brings happiness.

329   Let go of lost opportunities. There will always be
opportunities in your life that you didn't take, because you

didn't see them, because you were already committed, or because you valued something else more highly. Rather than cursing yourself for missing these opportunities, remember that you made the best choices you could at the time. Look ahead

and follow your chosen path, seeking the doorways that are
open to you and forgetting about those you have closed.

330   **Don't live in the past.** The past is a rich source of memories
and lessons, but if we spend all our time there we are unable to
appreciate the gifts that surround us in the present.

Even more important, **don't wish the past could be
different (331)**: it's a changeless vista. You might as well wish
that Mount Fuji was covered in mulberry trees. Understand the
value of your mistakes – they are a rich source of lessons that
help you to move forward with greater success in the future.

332   **Say the Serenity Prayer:** "God grant me Serenity to accept
the things I cannot change, Courage to change the things I can,
and Wisdom to know the difference."

333 **Be light.** To be light is different from being trivial, flippant or uncaring. Lightness is a graceful ability to dance triumphantly in the face of destiny – an approach to life that contrasts with the slow, lumbering weight of solemnity. Try to cultivate lightness for a while, but don't labour the point. Allow it to come to you as naturally as leaves to a tree.

334 **Just be good.** We don't need an opportunity to *do* good in order to *be* good! All doing begins with being. Being is doing to an enlightened soul. Being good means being positive when others choose to be negative, being open when others choose to be closed, being accepting when others opt for resistance. Goodness is a state of being – and it is stressless!

335 **Stop at enough.** "Do more", "achieve more", "acquire more" are the most mischievous mantras of the modern world. They represent a constant drive toward more than enough, creating a never-ending spiral of unfulfilled promise. Reject them, and be satisfied with all your assets and your endless potential.

336 **Ration your evenings out** to two or three evenings a week. By limiting your number of social engagements, you will appreciate them much more. Use your free evenings to pursue other interests, such as exercise, reading or creativity, and to recharge your batteries and your bank balance.

337 **Be a trustee, not an owner,** of your possessions. This subtle shift in perception frees you from fear of loss or damage.

338 **Use pen and paper,** the old-fashioned way, instead of using your computer. This links your words more directly with your thoughts, connects you with an honourable tradition, and gives your eyes and posture a break from the tyrannical screen.

Handwrite letters to friends and family (339) – it's much more personal than typing letters or emailing, and will be greatly appreciated by the recipient.

340 Avoid news overload.

Many of us bury our heads
in newspapers and news
magazines, because we feel a
responsibility to keep up with
current events. However, in a world of global communications
the brain can't absorb all the news available to us. To avoid
overload, select carefully what you want to read.

Instead of trying to keep up with all world events, **specialize
(341)** in two or three topics and follow them in depth.

Mark landmark news events (342) in your diary. This will
help you to see your own life in a broader historical perspective,
giving you a sense of proportion about your experiences.

343 Go on a mini-retreat for just one day, or for a morning or
afternoon. Ban the phone, the television and radio, and the car
(unless you need the car to transport you to your chosen place
of tranquility). Meditate and give thanks for your blessings.
Mindfully appreciate your time spent alone.

344   **Be kind to yourself.** As the Buddha wisely said, "If your compassion does not include yourself, it is incomplete." Be aware of the judgments that you cast upon yourself and gently seek to dismantle them.

345   **Reflect lovingly on yourself.** Imagine that you are sitting quietly by a still pool surrounded by palm trees and rocks. As you look down into the still water, you see your face reflected

there. Notice the calmness in your expression. As you gaze into your reflected eyes, you are struck by their serenity, their infinite capacity to love. Your reflection is content in your presence, and always happy to respond to your summons whenever you gaze into a mirror-like surface. It admires you. Return its esteem. Offer love to your own image.

346   Shower yourself with good wishes. Visualize yourself strolling through a dense jungle, then arriving at a pool into which a waterfall is flowing. Stand beneath the cascade of water, imagining that the spray is saturated with the blessings and good wishes of all the people in your life today. Resolve to say a silent thankyou with your eyes next time you see them.

347   Write a letter of appreciation to yourself, expressing yourself as if you were a stranger who has observed you from afar and is impressed by your personal qualities and achievements. You may be surprised how complimentary and convincing your letter of praise turns out to be.

348 **Give yourself a present on your birthday.** It's your special day, so treat yourself to a luxury of some kind – not necessarily something material, but perhaps a massage, or even just an extra hour of quiet time.

Alternatively, use your birthday as a pretext to **try something you've always wanted to do (349)** but have never found the time for – such as a hot-air balloon trip, or a Ferris wheel ride.

350 **Invite yourself round for dinner** and treat yourself to your favourite meal. After preparing the food and before dining, set the table with candles and flowers and change into fresh clothes – after all, it's a special occasion.

351 **Imagine you've been kidnapped** by the conspirators in a plot to eliminate all pain: they are truth, love and humour. Gazing steadfastly into your eyes, Truth reminds you that life is an adventure and should not be taken too seriously. Arms round your shoulders, Love shyly ventures that your spirit is dazzling. Then Humour shows up to tell your all-time favourite joke. You laugh again, as you have a thousand times before. Your laughter echoes around the world; all pain is vanquished.

352 **Star in your own movie.** Imagine that you are the writer, director and lead actor. The title of the film is *Relaxed, Happy and Loved*. The other characters comprise your family, friends, neighbours and colleagues. Play out the film in your head, providing suitable background music and special effects where required. It's the story of your life – the best movie you'll ever see. Write a glowing review of this masterpiece.

353 **Develop a personal success chart.** Draw up a chart showing the months of the year across the top and the different areas of your life down the side – relationships, work, creativity, personal development, health. At the end of each month, reflect on the successes that you have had in each area. This could be anything from completing a project at work to attending a regular dance class. For each achievement place a gold star in the relevant column to reward you for your efforts.

You could also create for yourself a **life chart (354)** to remind you of the achievements in your life thus far.

355   **Enjoy being your age.** You'll never be so young again! Appreciate your growing wisdom and experience – it would sit oddly with a younger body and face.

Remember, you can **feel young (356)**, and therefore *be* young, by remaining ever-curious about the world, open to new challenges and experiences.

357   **Celebrate wrinkles,** gray hairs and other small signs of aging. They reflect maturity. Wear them proudly – they are the badges of your wisdom and experience.

358   **Reclaim your power.** The opposite of a mentor is someone who overshadows your mental horizon, someone in whose presence you feel cowed. Imagine that person arriving on your doorstep one day. They have come to return your power. They hand you a gift-wrapped box. You accept this with thanks and

open it to find an orb of light. You absorb the orb into your
heart. You now have your power back. Why let them infect you
with their energy when you have infinite energy of your own?

359 **Speak up for your beliefs,** however unpopular you feel they may be. It's good to get into the habit of small-scale risk taking: it's essential to our growth and our ability to handle difficult situations. On the other side of risk is the quiet satisfaction that we have defeated our biggest enemy – our fear!

360 **Play your own true note.** St Augustine once said: "Make sure your life sings the same tune as your mouth." Any disparity between your words and your actions inevitably leads to inner tension. Be open and sincere. Talk your walk; walk your talk.

361 **Value the power of thought.** Reflect on the formidable creative powers of nature – caterpillars transforming into butterflies, new buds forming on a pruned tree. See your own ideas in a similar light: you have an infinite capacity to spin one idea out of another. You are the emperor of the world of thought.

362 **Create a positive thought about yourself,** such as "I am at peace" or "I am a loving soul". Then choose an object, link

the object with the thought, and meditate on
both together. Allow the object to open and
deepen the thought. For example, you might
link "I am at peace" with a teacup. Imagine
the cup filling with liquid peace. It overflows,
reminding you that your store of peace is infinite.
Imagine yourself handing the cup to a friend under
stress. You see them drink from your cup and smile.
Already they feel more relaxed – as are you.

363 **Play visualization golf** (or any other sport or game) – a
vivid image of your inward quest for peace. Imagine you are
stepping up to the first tee of your local golf course. See your
first drive fly straight and true down the middle. Your pitch to
the green soars high into the heavens and down, landing
perfectly, three feet from the hole. You relish the putt as the
ball drops in the cup. Enjoy the remaining seventeen holes in
the same way. It's the perfect round, leaving you with your
feet up at the "nineteenth" – a relaxing break in the clubhouse.

Body

TOUCH

364   **Discover the benefits of massage.** Scientific studies have shown that massage is one of the easiest ways to attain and maintain good health. On a physical level, massage increases the circulation, relaxes the muscles, aids digestion and stimulates the lymphatic system, thereby aiding elimination of waste from the body. On an emotional level, massage relaxes us and creates a sense of love, warmth and security.

365   **Exercise your hands** before massaging yourself or another to increase their flexibility and sensitivity. Start by vigorously rubbing the back of your left hand with the palm of the right. Repeat with the hands reversed. Then, rub your palms together until they feel hot. Finish by holding your palms together, then lifting your elbows up until your palms no longer touch. Press your fingers against each other and hold for 6 seconds, stretching the finger and wrist joints.

366   **Practise stroking** – this is the simplest massage technique and forms the basis of any massage. Concentrate on making the stroking movements flowing and rhythmic. Experiment with altering the speed and pressure to add variety: slow movements are calming; fast movements are stimulating. Mould your hands to the shape of the body and try to keep one hand in contact with the body throughout the massage.

As you become more confident, experiment with **kneading (367)** – a technique whereby you press the flesh firmly with the fingers, as though kneading dough. This technique is ideal for releasing tension in the shoulders and fleshy areas such as the hips and thighs.

At the end of a massage use stimulating **percussion movements (368)** to energize the person. Either form your hands into loose fists and, with relaxed wrists, bounce the sides of your fists alternately against the skin, or strike the skin with the sides of your hands, flicking them away as soon as you make contact. Use both hands alternately and work very quickly.

369   Massage with essential oils. Use a light vegetable oil, such as almond, grapeseed or soya, as a carrier for the essential oils, which are extremely concentrated. Dilute one to three drops of essential oil with a teaspoon of carrier oil. Using essential oils will help your hands glide smoothly over the skin, as well as bringing both giver and receiver the benefits of the essential oil (see point 466, page 197). For a basic massage oil, try lavender, which eases stress, relieving symptoms such as headaches, insomnia, nervous anxiety and mild depression.

370 Absorb yourself in the massage. Focus on the various sensations in your hands (if you are giving) or in your body (if you are receiving); allow yourself to be hypnotized by the rhythm of the strokes. In this way the massage becomes an active meditation, calming and relaxing to both parties.

371 Massage your face. Stress makes us unwittingly knot

our brows or clench our jaws.
Use your index and middle
fingers to iron out these
tensions. Start by making
circles on your brow,
moving from the middle
toward your temples. Then make sharp upward strokes along
the bridge of your nose. Finally, close your eyes and gently rest
the heels of your hands in your eye sockets. Do each of these
three stages for about a minute.

372 **Ease a headache** or migraine by applying gentle pressure
with the forefingers to the acupressure points that lie around the
eyes. There are seven of these: one between the two eyebrows
in the middle of the brow; two in the middle of the eyebrows;
two below these, halfway along the lower ridges of the eye-
sockets; two in the slight indentations at the outer edges of the
eye-sockets, next to the temples. For each point in turn, hold the
pressure for 3 seconds and then gently release.

373 **Release tension** in your scalp.
Grasp your hair close to the scalp
and squeeze several times by
clenching and releasing your fists.
Then, still grasping your hair by the roots, move
your fists backward and forward so that your scalp slides across
your skull. Repeat these actions all over your head.

374 **Relieve pain at the back of the head** by pressing with
your fingers on the acupressure points along the base of the
skull where tension is often stored. Start with the centre of
your neck and work outward to finish behind the ears.

375 **Treat tired feet.** Sit on a firm chair or stool with both feet
on the ground and place your left ankle on your right knee.
Then, gripping the outside of the foot with your right hand,
press your thumb firmly into the area just under the ball and
toward the middle. Maintain the pressure on this point for
about 10 seconds, then relax. Repeat on your right foot.

376   **Try a pebble foot massage** to relax and revive you after a long day. Cover the bottom of a shallow tub or bowl with a layer of round pebbles (or marbles). Pour half a cup of hot, salty water over it (as hot as you can handle) and add a few drops of your favourite essential oil (peppermint, with its antiseptic and cooling properties, is ideal for this). Put your feet in the tub and roll them over the pebbles, administering gentle pressure to your soles.

377   **Stroke a cat** or another furry animal. Studies have shown that stroking pets is theraputic, as unconditional love is exchanged through contact. It can also reduce high blood pressure.

378   **Plunge your hand into a bowl of lentils** or other beans. Swirl your hand through them and sift them through your fingers, relishing the soothing sensations produced by the textures.

379   **Wear a cashmere scarf** in cold weather. They're expensive, but wonderfully warm and soft against the skin.

ENERGY TECHNIQUES

380   **Connection shiatsu** remedies short, shallow breathing caused by stress. Lie on your back and place the palm of one hand on your abdomen, the palm of the other on your chest. Hold for one minute. This will stimulate the flow of *chi* (vital energy) between your lungs and your kidneys (the "seat" of anxiety), helping you to relax and breathe more deeply.

381   **Develop breath awareness.** There is a close relationship between the pattern of our breathing and our state of mind – breathing tends to be shallow and rapid when we are anxious, deep and slow when we are relaxed. By becoming more aware of our breathing, we can consciously alter the pattern to bring us to a more relaxed state of body and mind. Begin by lying on your back, eyes closed, breathing through your nose. Place one hand on your chest and one on your abdomen, and focus on your hands as they rise and fall, reflecting the rhythm and depth of your breathing.

     Lengthen the breath (382) if your hands are moving quickly. As you breathe in, slowly count up to four, and as you breathe out, slowly count up to six. On the second in-breath count up to five, and on the out-breath count up to seven. Continue increasing the lengths of your breaths until your in-breath reaches seven counts and your out-breath nine counts. Maintain this rate for ten breaths.

If you find that only the hand on your chest is moving, your breathing is too shallow. To help you **deepen the breath (383)** visualize it as light flowing down into your abdominal area and out again.

384   The humming-bee breath creates a sound like that of a bee. Humming causes a vibration in the body that is soothing and nurturing, bringing an overall sense of well-being. To practise this technique, sit in a comfortable position and take a long, steady in-breath. On the out-breath, hum gently, keeping your jaw relaxed. Continue to hum on every out-breath, allowing the sound to vibrate in the different areas of your face and head. Continue for eight to twelve breaths.

385 **Practise the victorious breath** (*ujjayi* breathing) to warm your body and develop your inner strength and willpower. Keeping your mouth closed, exhale and inhale through your nose. As you do so, slightly contract the muscles in your throat to

produce a gentle rushing sound
like the sound of the sea in a
seashell. Be careful not to
strain your breathing. Practise
this for twelve breaths, increasing
the number as you gain confidence.

386   **Roar like a lion.** Based on a yoga technique,
this is an excellent way to release tension and stress.
First take a deep breath, expanding your rib-cage as you
fill your lungs with air. Then open your mouth and throat
as wide as possible and expel the air by contracting your
stomach and diaphragm muscles. As you do so make an "Ahh"
sound – the louder and longer the better. Repeat three times,
allowing yourself to roar with greater force each time.

387   **Do a cat stretch** – a yoga posture that releases tension from
the spine, clearing the head and calming the nerves. Begin on
all fours with a neutral spine (neither arched down nor hunched),

shoulders over hands, hips over knees. As you breathe in, arch your back down and lift your chest and head slightly. As you breathe out, reverse the movement, curving your spine up and tilting your pelvis beneath you. Repeat this sequence six times.

388 **Relax your tongue.** Press your tongue against the roof of your mouth, hold it there for a few seconds, then relax. This exercise also helps to relieve tension in the jaw, neck and face.

389 **Breathe through your feet** to help you feel more grounded in times of stress. This exercise can be done whenever your feet are on the ground. As you inhale, imagine you are drawing in air through the soles of your feet, up through your legs and into your torso. As you exhale, imagine the reverse.

390 **Use polarity** to lift yourself out of lethargy. Lower your body into a squat with feet slightly apart. Shift your weight in a circular motion. Then rock gently to and fro. This facilitates energy flow by releasing tension in the pelvis.

391 **Lift your legs.** During inverted yoga postures, the blood rushes down toward the head, bathing the brain in life-giving oxygen. This can energize body and spirit. Lie on your back and lean your legs against a wall. Lightly clasp your hands a few inches above your head, on the floor. Your arms should form a diamond. Breathe deeply and evenly. Lie like this for 10 minutes. Performed before bedtime, this position is a good way to encourage restful sleep.

392 **Adopt the pose of the child** – a classic yoga resting posture. Based on the foetal position, this pose is calming and nurturing, and particularly helpful if you are experiencing difficult emotions, such as fear or anxiety. Begin by kneeling down, buttocks resting on your heels, with your spine straight and your arms by your sides. Exhaling, fold forward from your hips, bringing your chest to rest on your thighs and your forehead onto the floor. Let your hands slide back toward your feet and your arms rest on the floor. Close your eyes and breathe gently and evenly until any difficult feelings begin to subside.

FEEL RIGHT, LOOK RIGHT

393 **Ground yourself** using the basic yoga standing posture. Stand with feet parallel, a few inches apart, aware of contact between the soles of your feet and the earth. Distribute your weight evenly between the balls of your feet and your heels, and between right and left foot. Lengthen your legs by lifting your knees and thighs. Gently draw up your lower abdominal muscles and relax your shoulders and buttocks. Allow your arms to hang, relaxed, at your sides. Breathe deeply, smoothly and evenly.

394 **Visualize a golden thread** between the top of your head and the heavens. Think of it tightening and lifting you up, making your spine

straight, your shoulders lower and your rib-cage expand freely. Conjure this image whenever you feel yourself slouching.

395   **Photo raiders.** From time to time as you go about the day's business, imagine that two or three paparazzi have materialized from nowhere and are taking pictures of you. Consider what their photographs would say about you. Are there aspects of your posture you wouldn't wish your fans to see? Make any necessary adjustments to the way you are sitting or standing, and see if you can give them better pictures next time they pounce.

As a refinement on this, try using the **ringing of the phone (396)** as a signal for the paparazzi to press the shutter.

397   **Move slowly.** We often reveal our anxiety in fast, jerky move-ments. Slowing down can help calm our nerves. Remember, life is not a race. Some of the most profound experiences unfold slowly.

398   **Combat body consciousness** by seeing yourself as 1 per cent body, 99 per cent spirit. Value yourself from inside out, not outside in. Anyone whose opinion matters will accept your appearance and value you for your true inner qualities. Take pride in your appearance, by all means – just as you take pride in your home. But reject anxieties about any aspects of your body you cannot change.

399 **Pamper yourself.** The body is the vehicle for your spirit, so it's important to take care of it, nurturing it with regular cleansing, scrubbing and moisturizing. If you do this, you will look and feel healthier, which will boost your self-esteem.

For this reason, treat yourself to regular **haircuts (400)** and the occasional **pedicure (401)** if you fancy it.

EASY EXERCISE

402 **Power walking** – that is, walking at roughly twice the normal speed – is a healthy form of aerobic exercise that can be done en route to work or home, or in your lunch break (you'll need a change of clothes). Or you could do it in a park or in the countryside for a more liberating experience. Between 20 and 30 minutes is the optimum time.

403 **Go for a jog,** preferably around a park or in the countryside to avoid inhaling toxic traffic fumes. As you run, allow yourself to be soothed by the pounding rhythm of your feet. Take time to appreciate your surroundings rather than absorbing yourself entirely in your own thoughts.

404 **Skip with a rope** on your patio, backyard or lawn. Although this is an energetic activity, the repetitiveness of the movement and the swinging of the rope have a lulling effect on the body. Reminiscent of the rhyming chants of childhood, jumping rope can transport you back to the innocent play of schooldays.

405 **Skip down a gentle hill.** The combination of fine views, energetic and joyful movement and the sense of soaring into the air with each downward leap makes this a particularly exhilarating way to relax.

406 **Climb a mountain.** Although this is commonly a metaphor for major achievement, not all mountains are hard to scale – all you need is a road or cablecar to give you a good start, then a clear path to the summit. Take plenty of time to

appreciate the views from the top. Perform a 5-minute meditation on each of the four cardinal views (that is, looking north, south, east and west). Relish the privilege of altitude.

Sing as you climb (407) – this will help you to maintain a steady pace, and offers a great opportunity for singing your heart out to the world. You may also find that it forges a bond between you and the other climbers in your group.

If you are spiritually inclined, do a **mountain pilgrimage (408)**, regarding each step taken toward the summit as a sign of spiritual commitment. The view from the top provides a foretaste of the heights you'll scale if you persist in your spiritual journey.

409 **Go swimming.** Of all sports, swimming probably places least strain on the body – whatever speed you swim, the water will support you, preventing muscle strain or joint injury and allowing you to relax into the movement. Enjoy the sense of weightlessness as you float and the sense of power as you cleave the water.

If you feel at home in water you may enjoy **scuba-diving (410)**, which allows you to explore the magical worlds that co-exist with our own, beneath the water's surface.

411 **Go skiing** – an exhilarating sport that combines breathtaking scenery with the excitement and release of speed. The challenge is to overcome your fear and lean down the mountain, trusting yourself enough to surrender to the pull of gravity.

If the pace of downhill skiing does not appeal, you might prefer **cross-country skiing (412)**, which tests strength and stamina while bringing the rewards of stunning scenery, increased fitness and a sense of inner satisfaction.

413 **Go for a cycle ride.** If you have access to suitable terrain, cycling can be a wonderfully relaxing activity that allows you to travel further than if you were walking or running, without placing undue strain on the body. It is therefore an ideal way of exploring new places. The flat, sinuous curves of a riverbank are ideal cycling territory and often provide lovely scenery to delight you along the way.

If you like to relax your mind by challenging your body, try **mountain biking (414)** with its tough ascents, rewarded by spectacular views and exhilarating downhill stretches.

415 **Learn hatha yoga** – a form of exercise which aims to unite body, mind and spirit through breath-work and physical postures. A spiritual practice rather than a sport, yoga is not competitive, so work at your own pace and level of suppleness.

If you prefer something less physically demanding, try the Chinese art of **tai chi (416)** , in which you work with the energies of the body through slow sequences of continuous movement.

FOOD AND DRINK

417 **Drink lots of water.** Have at least six glasses of filtered, bottled or distilled water daily. This will help flush out impurities and prevent energy-sapping dehydration. A lack of water can seriously affect the function of all our bodily systems, leading to problems such as dry skin, headaches and poor concentration, to name but a few.

If you opt for bottled water, do a **mineral water tasting (418)**: you may be surprised by how different they taste, depending on their source and the method of treatment. Buy a number of different types and decide which one you prefer.

419 **Eat fruit and vegetables every day.** They bring you into contact with the energies of sun and earth, as well as providing vital nutrients and boosting the immune system.

Buy local farm-fresh food (420). Most supermarket produce is stored in warehouses and then shipped over from destinations all around the world before it reaches our shelves. During this time, the nutrient content of the food has often deteriorated. Buying farm-fresh produce ensures that your food is as nutritious as possible, as well as supporting local farmers.

Buy organic foods (421). Although expensive, organic foods are generally free of the pesticide and fertilizer residues that damage health. They also tend to be richer in immune-boosting phytonutrients because they have not been grown in the depleted soils used for standard varieties.

422 **Eat pineapple and papaya,** which are rich in the protein-digesting enzymes bromelain and papain respectively.

423 **Foods to calm you down** include cottage cheese, pasta, avocados, bananas and skimmed milk. All are rich in a protein

called tryptophan, which the body uses to make serotonin – a hormone that regulates our sleep and boosts our mood.

424 **Cut down on processed foods** – these are generally a source of "empty" calories, being high in fat and sugar and low in fibre and nutrients. Furthermore, most processed foods contain additives and preservatives, some of which have been clinically proven to cause behavioural disturbances in children and adults.

In particular, **avoid monosodium glutamate (425)** – a food additive that causes insomnia and headaches in certain people.

426 **Stabilize your blood-sugar levels** by eating five or six small meals a day. This helps your body to cope with stress by reducing the burden on the adrenal glands (responsible for releasing the stress hormone cortisol) and regulating levels of the feel-good hormones – serotonin and dopamine.

For the same reason, **avoid stimulants (427)**, such as coffee, tea and cigarettes, and **depressants (428)**, such as alcohol – all of which cause dramatic blood-sugar lurches.

Eat foods containing plenty of **fibre and protein (429)** (which release their sugar slowly) to compensate for any starchy or sugary foods (which are faster-releasing and therefore more likely to cause peaks and then troughs in your blood-sugar levels).

430 **Drink fluids between rather than during meals** as they
can reduce the absorption of nutrients and can upset digestion.

431 **Adapt your diet to the season.** In winter, eat heart-
warming cooked foods, and in summer opt for lighter meals
containing plenty of raw fruit and vegetables.

432 **Avoid combining starches and proteins in the same
meal** to optimize your digestion. This is because starch and
protein require different digestive conditions – the enzymes
that break down protein function best in a more acidic
environment, whereas the enzymes that digest starch
operate in a more alkaline environment.

   If this is unavoidable, follow the example of birds by
stacking your foods (433) so that within a single
meal you eat proteins first and then starches.

434 **Make a meal for a friend.** Often those
most in need of nourishment – the sick and

infirm – are unable to cook or go shopping. Make a wholesome meal for a friend in need and deliver it to them. It is good karma to support the physical and emotional needs of others.

435 **Eat little and often,** avoiding heavy meals, which place a much greater burden on your digestive system.

436 **Avoid stocking up on food when hungry.** If you do, you may end up buying more than you need, which in turn will encourage you to overeat or throw food away.

437 **Eat slowly,** relishing every mouthful. Give full attention to the textures and tastes of the food. Appreciate the ambience of the setting – whether familiar or otherwise. This is the body's time: treat your hunger and its satisfaction with respect.

About 10 per cent of our daily energy is spent on the digestion, absorption and metabolism of food. After meals, **give yourself some quiet time (438)** to allow these processes to take place unimpeded.

439 **Cook a meal with love** – remembering that cooking is creative, and deeply symbolic of the tides of your heart. Our thoughts go into whatever we cook, so it's good to have loving and peaceful thoughts while preparing a meal. Without them all we are doing is refuelling.

440 **Start a cookery club with friends.** This might involve a rotation system, whereby once a month one member of the group cooks a meal for all the others. The meals could be themed according to the cook's most recent vacation or a slip of paper bearing the name of the cuisine, picked at random out of a hat. This formal arrangement (which doesn't mean that the atmosphere need be formal) has the advantage of encouraging each cook to experiment with exotic and memorable dishes.

441 **Invent a recipe** using at least one ingredient that you have never previously cooked with. Relish the new textures, smells and tastes. If your meal is a success, you can cook it in the future; if not, you can laugh about it with your housemates.

442   **Make colourful ice cubes** by freezing pieces of fruit in the water, or by juicing and then freezing them. The ice cubes will turn a regular glass of mineral water into a special summer drink – a delightful treat for yourself and any guests.

443   **Make your favourite childhood** meal for yourself, particularly if you are feeling vulnerable and in need of some comfort and reassurance. It may release all kinds of fascinating memories of distant childhood days.

444   **Bake a cake.** Don't rush the task: enjoy the preparation and use the actual baking time for quiet reflection. Why not **surprise your friend or partner (445)** with their favourite cake? Taking the time and care to prepare a personal treat for them will lovingly express your appreciation of them.

446   **Enjoy chocolate.** The main constituent of chocolate is cocoa – a substance first consumed by the Aztecs, who recognized its stimulating and restorative properties, reserving it for warriors, priests and nobles. Today cocoa is known to be rich in antioxidants, which protect us from cancer-promoting free radicals. Good-quality chocolate tends to be high in cocoa and low in sugar, so you can nibble it without feeling guilty.

447   **Make your own bread.** Take out any stress on the dough with vigorous kneading; later, reap the fruits of your efforts with a slice of deliciously scented, freshly-baked bread.

448   **Perform a tea ceremony** to transform your afternoon teatime into a meditative ritual. Make the tea slowly and deliberately, using the best tea-set you have. Lay everything out with precision, and with a due sense of everyday sacredness. Take long pauses between each movement, particularly the drinking. Be totally mindful of every movement. You may be surprised to find that such a ceremony has a deeply calming effect. Once you have mastered your personal tea ceremony, invite some friends to join you. Drink tea together in silence.

To enhance the calm induced by this ritual, experiment with alternative teas: **green tea (449)** is soothing and caffeine-free; **liquorice tea (450)** helps to support adrenal function, thereby reducing stress; and **peppermint (451)** and **ginger teas (452)** calm the digestive tract and stomach.

453 **Peel an apple in a single strip.** Perform the task slowly, trying to keep the strip thin and of even width. Giving your full concentration to this task will sharpen your senses and clear your mind, enhancing your enjoyment of the apple when you eat it.

BODY WISDOM

454   **Take responsibility for your own health.** There is a Western tendency to see disease as something to which we fall victim – the disease attacks us and there is nothing we can do to defend ourselves. In fact there is plenty we can do. Taking care of our bodies is perhaps the most important thing. This may seem obvious but all too often we deprive the body of sleep, fuel it with junk food, pollute it with cigarettes and alcohol, fail to exercise it, and then are surprised when the body starts to break down, having lost its ability to fend off disease. To improve our health it is important to look honestly at the ways we mistreat our bodies, and then work to alter those habits.

One way to look after the body is to undergo a **regular health assessment (455)** with a health practitioner – orthodox or complementary – to catch problems early before they develop. If this seems excessive, consider that you would probably give your car an annual service, so why not your body?

For the same reason, go for **regular eye-tests (456)** and **dental check-ups (457)**. The eye-test is particularly important if you spend much of your time working at a computer – an activity that can strain the eyes. The dental check-up will ward off decay and gum disease, and keep staining to a minimum.

458 **Detox yourself** once a year for a period of four weeks. In the first week eliminate all dairy and wheat-based products from your diet, reduce your salt in-take, avoid meat and animal fat, tea, coffee, refined sugar, alcohol and tobacco. Instead, fill your diet with plenty of fresh fruit and vegetables, fish, brown rice, lentils, beans, millet, buckwheat flour, fresh herbs, and herbal teas such as ginger, peppermint, camomile and fennel.

Balance your meals: **eat well in the morning and at lunchtime (459)** to provide you with enough energy to get through the day. By contrast, your dinner should be very light and preferably eaten before seven o'clock in the evening.

While following this diet, **drink plenty of filtered, bottled or mineral water (460)** and **go to bed earlier (461)** than usual. In the third week, introduce a program of **low-intensity exercise (462)**, performed twice daily for 45 minutes each time, to assist the detoxification.

463 **Supplement your diet** with daily doses of vitamins C and B-complex if you feel stressed on a regular basis: vitamin C is vital for the production of anti-stress hormones; while vitamin B-complex, known as the "morale vitamin", has a beneficial effect on the nervous system and on mental attitude.

In addition to vitamins, there are a number of **flower essences (464)** and **herbal remedies (465)** – available from most good health stores – which, if taken wisely, can help bring balance and calm to your daily routine. Australian Bush Flower Essences and their English counterparts, Bach Flower Essences, are a subtle but effective way of correcting all sorts of emotional imbalances. The herbal remedy, St John's Wort, works by increasing

the levels of serotonin in circulation in the body and is one
of the most widely prescribed antidepressants in Germany;
similarly, kava-kava has been proven to help reduce stress
by promoting a clear mind and a sense of inner calm.

466 Visit an aromatherapist. Practitioners of aromatherapy use
the concentrated essential oils of plants to relieve a range of
emotional and physical conditions, including those that are
stress-related. These oils can be used alone or in blends for
massage, inhalation, compresses, baths and in special burners.

If you want to experiment with essential oils on your own, try
the following, which are particularly beneficial for relaxation:
fruity and apple-like in scent, **camomile (467)** soothes the
nerves and is suitable for sensitive skin; sweet-smelling **jasmine
(468)** acts as an antidepressant, and is particularly helpful for
the treatment of post-natal depression; **lavender (469)**, which
has a fresh fragrance, has antiseptic, analgesic and calming
properties, and can be used to treat headaches, insomnia and
depression; **petitgrain (470)** has a sweet aroma and acts as a

sedative and treatment for anxiety and insomnia; exotic **ylang ylang (471)** has antidepressant, sedative and antiseptic properties and helps to allay anxiety. You can dilute these (or other essential oils) in a carrier oil for massage (see point 369, page 161), place a few drops in the bath (see point 964, page 358) or on a pillow, or buy an oil burner to scent your bedroom.

472   **Recover properly** from illness, even if you have to take time off work or cancel plans. Don't feel guilty if you let people down: you need to take care of yourself in order to take care of others.

473   **Know your body clock.** We all have different natural phases of high and low energy. If you recognize these and do high-energy and low-energy tasks at the appropriate times, you will make the most of your day, both creatively and practically.

474   **Overcome winter blues.** During dark winter months it's common to suffer from fatigue, irritability and attention lapses. These are the symptoms of SAD (seasonal affective disorder) – a hormonal imbalance that occurs as a result of inadequate exposure to natural light. The cure is to spend no less than one hour a day outside, and to install full-spectrum lamps indoors.

475 **Balance female hormones naturally** by eating estrogenic foods such as soya, tofu, sweet potatoes, broccoli, cauliflower and Brussels sprouts. This will help tackle the symptoms of PMS (pre-menstrual syndrome), such as mood swings, headaches, breast pain and water retention, that afflict many women each month.

Other helpful measures that you can take just before your period include **cutting down on foods with high salt content (476)**, such as pretzels, salted peanuts and processed meats; and **taking a high-strength vitamin B complex (477)** to help your liver process estrogens, **vitamin E, calcium and magnesium (478)** to help to reduce the symptoms of tension and keep you calm, and **GLA (479)** (gamma linoleic acid), which is found abundantly in evening primrose oil, to reduce breast pain.

The peaceful home

LIGHT, SHADE AND COLOUR

480 **Use mirrors** to maximize the flow of energizing natural light through your home. Light promotes physical vitality and mental alertness. Its absence can cause vitamin D deficiencies, as well as fatigue, depression or irritability. What better antidote than a few mirrors carefully positioned to illuminate dark corners?

Many people prefer to **avoid seeing reflections (481)** of themselves as they move around the house or apartment. This problem is usually easy to solve by angling mirrors downward; or positioning them at higher or lower levels than your eyes; or just by judging the sightlines carefully.

Another approach is to **place a potted plant in front of a mirror (482)**. This spreads the light while at the same time fragmenting unwanted reflections. It also has the advantage of doubling the impact of the plant. Use hinged mirrors to increase the multiplication even further.

483 **Install a skylight** or dormer window if possible in an attic room used as a study or home office: you'll really enjoy the all-day natural light.

484 **Follow the sun** on its journey around the room on a sunny day. Notice how the light quality changes depending on the angle at which sunlight falls through the window. Plan your interior décor to make the most of such daily and seasonal changes. The peaceful home is one that you have created around the given cycles of natural lighting.

485 **Use sheer fabrics** as curtains or shades to diffuse and soften the light where appropriate (for example, in living rooms and possibly dining rooms), creating an ethereal mood that combines seclusion and mystery.

In other rooms (such as bedrooms) you might choose instead to **use thick drapes or shutters (486)** to allow you to block out daylight completely, helping you to generate an intimate, relaxing mood.

487 **Opt for flexible artificial lighting** – not just a single light source but a number of alternative light sources at different heights in every room. The ideal is to have a choice of lighting permutations, including individual pools of light around chairs and occasional tables, some directional lighting (for example, to provide good light to work by), and some light purely for ambient mood.

Employ a professional (488) to install the optimum lighting. This might seem like an expensive undertaking, and potentially a stressful one, involving some redecoration as well as purely technical rewiring work. However, the financial investment is well worthwhile, as this is one of the most effective ways to control your home environment and match it to your moods from hour to hour – almost certainly a major key to achieving the peaceful home.

Fit dimmer switches (489) to increase your range of lighting options further.

490 **Use directional lighting** to highlight or dramatize favourite objects, such as sculptural forms, pictures or the room's most striking fabrics. This helps to make a room appear more personalized and therefore more welcoming. Carved figures in

stone, wood or other materials often look great when narrow sidelighting is used to emphasize their contours with a pattern of shadows and highlights.

Picture lighting (491) may be provided by a small uplighter in a special brass attachment set within a picture frame; or alternatively a floor-standing spotlight. To highlight a lovely landscape in this way allows the picture to exert its subtly relaxing influence even when the room lights are turned down low.

492   **Candles** offer a wonderful source of mood lighting – as well as a suitable focus for a simple meditation (see point 245, page 111). Look out for interesting holders, such as pierced-tin cylinders, which can cast a soothing light show onto nearby walls.

You can also **float candles (493)** in decorative bowls filled with water to establish an ambience of gentle mysticism.

(Never leave a candle unattended; and be sure that the flame is at a safe distance from any object or material, whether flammable or not.)

494 **Use colours strategically,** bearing in mind their impact on mood. Cooler hues tend to be calming, warmer hues tend to be stimulating. Bear in mind the psychological and spiritual meanings associated with colours:

Red (495) is associated with fire, so that a patch of red in a room can be a subtle substitute for a blazing hearth.

Orange (496) is linked with spirituality and transcendence, and is a good colour for meditators.

Yellow (497), associated with sunlight, promotes optimism.

Green (498) connects us with nature and instils a sense of harmony.

Blue (499), the colour of an untroubled sky, suggests openness, freedom and tranquility.

Indigo (500), reminiscent of

ocean depths, adds mystery to an interior.

Violet (501), symbolic of the "inner eye", the centre of spiritual vision, can guide us on the inward quest.

502 **Use cushions** in different hues to add changeable accents of colour to suit your mood at any particular time.

503 **White walls** suggest purity, creating a look of almost monastic asceticism that is conducive to mental clarity.

504 **Mix hues judiciously** to create a harmonious effect – either different colours in matching tones or a narrower range of colours in different tones. Neutral hues, such as off-whites, creams, buffs or grays, provide a subdued background to off-set splashes of more vibrant hue – a safe option for those who are uncertain of their colour sense.

505 **Use patterns with restraint** – too many patterns of different kinds may clash with each other and subtly disturb your mental equilibrium. On the other hand, **rich patterns (506)** can conjure up calm through their associations with nature or with a pre-industrial lifestyle. Many patterns are Eastern in origin (think of Eastern carpets), and so conjure up a relaxed ambience for Westerners inspired by Eastern wisdom.

   Stencil-paint leaves or flowers (507) onto a plain wall to conjure up a tranquil rustic setting.

MANAGING YOUR SPACES

508   **Clear out your clutter.** Sorting out your wardrobes, drawers
and cupboards and throwing out all that accumulated rubbish
will allow the things you need and treasure to breathe. Above
all, you'll know that there's order even in hidden places –
a good analogy for the virtue that shines within the spirit.

509   **Visit the local dump** about twice a year to get rid of those
bulky objects that are an eyesore every time you catch sight of
them. Make an occasion of it: take a picnic, or celebrate
afterwards in whatever way takes your fancy.

510   **Give to a thrift store** or charity collection – a great way
to combine a clear-out with a generous civic gesture. Wash any
clothes before you give them away; mend any tears; replace
any missing buttons – all these selfless acts will increase the
karmic value of your donation.

511   **Recycle.** The amount of waste that we produce stresses the
planet and disrupts our links with nature. Recycle your paper,

bottles and cans, but most importantly recycle your thinking, and build a responsible relationship with the Earth.

512 **Blitz your backlog of chores,** starting early one morning, straight after an early breakfast. Working hard right up to mid-morning snack time guarantees that you'll feel good about yourself. Any downtime you take from this point onward will be doubly relaxing because thoroughly deserved.

513 **Swap chores with your partner,** for variety's sake. You might find that the fresh eye he or she brings to your regular household routines reveals more efficient or more enjoyable ways of doing things.

514 **When a friend comes round** to your place, get them to help you with little jobs that two can do better than one – for example, changing the duvet covers: it makes a change from doing it with your partner. And **when cooking for a friend (515),** why not ask them round early and get them to

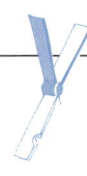

help you? A true friend with time to spare will always take pleasure in the opportunity to assist in the preparation of the meal and at the same time have a quiet chat with you.

516 **Do laundry mindfully** and turn a household chore into a kind of meditation exercise. When the clothes come from the dryer, enjoy the feel and the fresh smell of the warm fabric as you fold each item. If done with attention to detail, by the time your task is finished you should be feeling thoroughly peaceful and relaxed.

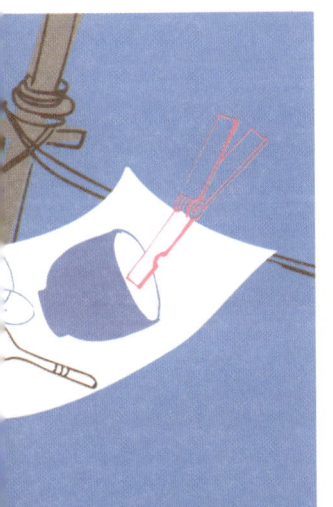

517 **Use clothes-pegs** to give a fun dimension to your "to do" list when household chores have begun to accumulate alarmingly and you don't know where to start. Write the tasks down on individual sheets of paper and hang each sheet on the clothes-line with a peg. Now pick and detach one of the sheets at random and complete the task that's written on it. As you perform the

tasks throughout the day, you'll see these job flags disappearing in a satisfying visual expression of your own productivity.

518 **Repair things** when possible, especially clothes: today we live in a throwaway culture, but our unwillingness to tolerate even minor imperfections is an unfortunate attachment. Take a more relaxed attitude and make do with things that are less than pristine but still in perfect working order.

For example, **darn your socks (519)** – every sock with a tiny hole in it is a potential source of good feelings if only you'd get out your darning kit. Do things properly, because that way it's more satisfying: for example, match replacement buttons perfectly, and use the right shade of thread.

520 **Learn sewing skills,** so that you can do more ambitious repairs. Sewing in a spirit of mindful attentiveness is a relaxing, almost meditative activity. Patch holes, hem trousers, replace worn pockets ... and so on.

521 **Have a tiny job day.** Do all the niggling little chores around the house that are pricking your conscience on a daily basis. Knocking off half a dozen or so little jobs on the same day is a certain way to nurture good feelings about yourself.

522 **Touch up the paintwork.** A few hours spent spot-treating scuffs and marks will enhance your home environment and subtly boost your peace of mind.

523 **Clean your windows.** Smears or other marks on glass may be a trivial blemish, but they interpose themselves between yourself and the outside world and are thus a constant reminder of minor neglect and therefore subliminally stressful. Use a squeegee or paper towels with a proprietary window cleaner. Wash the inside surface with up-and-down swipes and the outside with cross swipes: that way if a streak remains, you'll know which side of the glass it's on.

524 **Iron out your creases.** Even the most mundane of tasks, such as ironing, can be a exercise in calm. Imagine as you iron that the creases in your clothes are worries about life's insolubles. As you smooth out each crease, visualize one of these worries losing its sharp edges.

525 **Treat your car well** – it's small enough for you to be able to maintain it as a totally clean and clutter-free environment. Given the hours you spend driving, this is a much more relaxing approach than treating your car as a dump to carry the overspill of household clutter. Respect the car's inner needs, too: have it serviced regularly; fix minor mishaps (like a broken wing mirror) as soon as you can, though without getting stressed about it.

526 **Rearrange the furniture.** Experiment with new circulation routes. Break the grip of habit upon your domestic surroundings. Unless you set aside time to put deliberate thought into the optimum arrangement for your needs, you may miss good opportunities for making the home more user-friendly.

527 **Effective storage** of tools, appliances and materials is another key to the peaceful home. It's a good feeling when you open a cupboard and find what you need. Keep similar things together as much as possible.

528 **Read the instructions** properly the first time you use a new piece of equipment. Sit down and study them over a soothing beverage before you start. Rushing into things before you're properly prepared is a shortcut to stress.

POSITIVE ENERGIES

529   **Circulation routes,** such as halls, landings and stairs, are like the meridians, or energy lines, that thread through the body carrying *chi* (vital energy): both must be kept clear of blockages if the energy is to flow naturally. So avoid clutter in these parts of the home and place a ban on oversized furniture.

530   **Keep the middle of a room clear** to create a sense of spaciousness and energy. This is an important principle of Vastu Vidya (the ancient Indian spiritual tradition of architecture and placement), which asserts that furniture placed in the sacred centre of a room impedes the flow of energy (*prana*) through the space.

531   **The shape of your dining table,** according to Vedic principles, affects the ambience of the room. Square or rectangular represents the Earth element, and thus has a grounding effect. Circular represents the Water element, prompting lively conviviality. You may not be able to switch easily, but it's good to know what influences are afoot!

532 **Keep a chest within an alcove,** as the Japanese often do. Various precious objects for display are kept inside the chest, but only one piece is exhibited on top – rotate the piece at intervals, so you never get bored with the display.

533 **Orient your bed** so that your head points south when you sleep. According to the Indian tradition of Vastu Vidya (see point 530, opposite), the body possesses an electromagnetic field like a magnet, with the head as the north pole. Aligning this with the electromagnetic field of the Earth is believed to promote restful sleep. As opposite poles attract, this involves positioning your bed so that your head points toward the south pole.

534 **Improve air quality** in your home. According to the US Environmental Agency, the concentration of toxins can be more than 200 times greater inside buildings than outside. The prime requisite is to keep the home well ventilated by opening windows regularly: contrary to what you might expect, this will reduce the likelihood of colds and 'flu. Be sure to **avoid**

overheating (535) the home, and **use house plants (536)** as a means of filtering the air. If central heating and good insulation make the atmosphere too dry, water in unglazed terracotta vessels above or near radiators will help to redress the balance. Additional measures you can take to cleanse your domestic air supply and make the home environment healthier, and therefore more relaxing, include:

Use fewer chemical products (537). For example, air fresheners disguise nasty smells by releasing a chemical to coat the nasal passages with an oily shield or by dulling the olfactory nerves. Use herbs, not aerosols, to scent the air.

Use natural materials (538) wherever possible for furnishings or decoration.

Ban smoking (539) – visitors may smoke in the garden or backyard if they can't control their habit.

Use air ionizers (540) to boost the level of negative ions (electrically charged atoms) in the air. These offset the positive ion charge generated by heating systems and other equipment, which can create

fatigue, lethargy and
susceptibility to illness.

**541 Natural items in
a bathroom,** such
as seashells, driftwood,
stones and natural
sponges, give off
positive energies as
well as compensate,
in many bathrooms,
for the lack of a view.

542 Rescue harmless insects trapped in your house, instead of
thoughtlessly despatching them – they weren't trying to walk off
with your silver! Respect nature, even when it trespasses.

543 Crystals placed around your home will absorb negativity and
promote a happy, harmonious atmosphere. Choose crystals that

are rough-cut rather than polished. Before arranging them in the home, place them outside in a bowl of water for 24 hours: this practice cleanses and re-energizes the crystals, and should be repeated every month or so. The fascination of crystals comes from their earth-born beauty; but, in addition, they are a powerful metaphor for the spirit's transcendence of the flesh, or at a more mundane level the potential for transformation in all of us. Here are some brief profiles of some of the most popular types:

Clear quartz (544), also known as "white quartz" or "rock crystal", can lift us into a lighter, more joyful state.

Aventurine (545), a beautiful green stone, clears turbulent thoughts and purifies the emotions.

Rose quartz (546), associated with love, gently releases emotional blockages.

Yellow calcite (547) can help to lift our spirits out of depression, bringing inner strength and peace.

548 **A glass prism** placed on a window sill can make an ever-changing dance of light that is relaxing to watch.
Alternatively, use **coloured bottles (549)** filled with water to create a similarly soothing effect.

550 **Make a household altar.** Houses in ancient Rome often had a shrine to the household gods. Often the twins Castor and Pollux filled this role. Meditate on the twin qualities that give your home its character. Perhaps you have a strong relationship with particular saints or heroes. Equally, you might choose "welcome" and "rest", or "hearth" and "renewal". Combine pictures and objects that summarize your home's *genius loci* ("spirit of place"). The hearth, of course, is a good place for this.

551 **Burn incense.** Use aromas such as frankincense and sandalwood to create a positive yet relaxing ambience.

THE FEEL-GOOD HOME

552   **Name your house or apartment.** Choose a name that conjures up a positive image – for example, connoting calm, or strength, or inspiration. The subtle aura of the name will embrace you as you re-enter the home.

553   **A symbol of tranquility** in your entrance hall or just outside your front door will remind you to unwind when you come home. Consider hanging a plaque inscribed with a Chinese character, or an image of a dove. Pay respect to the emblem as you pass by.

   A symbol of longevity (554) also makes a good focal point for an entranceway, and there are many to choose from, especially in traditional Chinese belief. Examples are: the crane, a bird thought by the Chinese to live for a thousand years or more; the phoenix, the legendary bird that supposedly renewed itself in fire; the carp (which in its ornamental form can, of course, be embodied as real fish in a suitable pool); and the hare, elephant, deer, stork, toad, tortoise, turtle and peach. The colour green and the stone jade have similar connotations.

Symbols of abundance (555), such as the pomegranate and the cornucopia (horn of plenty), would also be suitable in this position.

556 **Welcome yourself** as you come home (as well as welcoming guests, of course) with a display of container plants at either side of your front door.

By using **pots of herbs (557)** you can combine a visual with an olfactory salute.

Once inside the home, you can create a convivial atmosphere with **freshly cut flowers (558)** placed in a vase in your hall.

For the Chinese, chrysanthemums are considered particularly good flowers for relaxation and will bring laughter and happiness into your home. Scented houseplants, such as jasmine or hyacinth, also make effective choices for hallways, defeating expectation by making the inside of the home smell as sweet as the garden.

559 Wear slippers at home – keep them by the front door so that you can slip into them when you enter. You might even consider having different pairs of slippers for different rooms of the house – the ultimate in Zen-like respect for floor surfaces.

560 Re-record your answer machine message regularly, making it positive and welcoming.

561 The silent world of an aquarium can be very soothing to watch. Many of the smaller freshwater schooling fish are good first choices, as they are both hardy and vivid. They include White Cloud Mountain Minnows, Danios, and Rasboras, all of which do better in groups of at least six of their own species.

562 A landscape painting or print will bring a refreshing openness – literally, an expansion of horizons – to any interior, as well as a mood of pastoral tranquility. Good options include:

Rustic scenes (563), perhaps showing country pursuits such as haymaking.

Sublime wilderness landscapes (564) in the manner of the German Romantic painter Caspar David Friedrich.

Snowscapes (565), to remind us of home comforts.

Images of **ancient Egypt (566)**, which suggest an exotic spirituality, especially if they feature the Pyramids or the Sphinx.

567 **Hang a stained glass decoration** inside a window to throw patterns of rainbow-hued light into the room whenever the sun catches the panels.

568 **Buy a kelim** – fix it to the wall and use its bold, abstract patterns as a focus for meditation. Alternatively place it on the floor and use it as a meditation mat.

569 **Introduce curves** into a room, for a softening effect. Curved shapes are gentler on the eye than angular ones, and invite repose. They can be three-dimensional (as in a round side-table

with scrolled feet) or two-dimensional (as in a pattern on fabric
or wallpaper).

570   **Still-lifes of found objects,** such as driftwood, stones, even
pieces of glass, not only make a focus for contemplation – for
example, on a low coffee table – but also evoke the walk when
you found them, thus conjuring up leisure time. Such relics of
the world outside help to ground a room in nature. Other
examples might include rough-hewn logs stored in a bucket,
smooth pebbles in simple bowls, feathers arranged on a tray.

To evoke the forest, make a **collection of cones and nuts
(571)**, displayed in a shallow bowl. With a little ingenuity you
can evoke seaside and mountain habitats in similar ways.

572   **Reflect the seasons.** Bring into your home the tones
and textures of nature to reflect the changing seasons, using
candles, and scents, plants and flowers that embody these times
of year. Spring is fresh and soft; summer, heady and bright;
autumn, darker and more abundant; winter, rich and heavy.

573 **Make a pot pourri** using the leaves of dried herbs or dried flower petals. Choose from the following: sage, pine, bergamot, bay, rosemary, rose geranium, fragrant roses, lavender, lemon verbena, peppermint. Mix in an attractive bowl with ground cloves or cinnamon, with a little ground orris root added as a preservative. Stir the pot pourri occasionally to release the scents. Revive it from time to time by sprinkling with a few drops of an essential oil.

574 **Freshen the air** with a custom-filled spray bottle. Fill the reservoir with water and then add about ten drops of an essential oil. To use, just squirt two or three times.

575 **Turn down the radio** from time to time so that you can hear the voices but not what they are saying – the volume should be quiet enough to create a low, soothing murmur.

576 **Humanize the hearth.** Make it not only the focal point of the room but a place of warm associations. **Candles (577)**, even

when unlit, immediately suggest traditional homeliness.
Family photos (578) can also add emotional warmth: buy a
multi-mount photo frame to display your loved ones as a group.

579 **Make a real fire in your fireplace** – provided, of course,
that you have a fully-operational chimney. Get
mindfully absorbed in tending the fire – feeding it,
and adjusting the coals or logs with a poker.
Relish the smells given off by different types of
firewood. (Choose firewood from a sustainable
source. And note that firewood must be
seasoned for at least 6 months to reduce
its water content. Green – that is, unsea-
soned wood – smokes a lot and causes a
build-up of creosote in the chimney.)

580 **Make a quilt of love** – a patchwork
quilt using patches of fabric that hold special meaning for you, such as a square of

your father's checked shirt, a cushion cover from your first marital home, and so on. This project combines the relaxing activity of sewing, the magpie pleasures of improvised assembly, and the celebratory instinct. Once the quilt is completed, you'll be able to wrap yourself in happy memories every night.

Make a toddler's quilt (581) using, for the patches, the child's clothes at different ages. The child is almost bound to respond well as you point out these evocative souvenirs of his or her own past.

582 **Do some gardening.** The physical exercise combined with the involvement with nature will release tension. Vary the task according to your state of mind – serious digging when you feel like a work-out; gentle weeding when you're more spiritually inclined. And don't forget to enjoy the garden's beauties while you work.

583 **Weed the garden** by hand. If you wish, you can turn your weeding into a checklist of inner resolutions, ticking off the elimination of a bad habit with every errant plant you uproot.

584 **Plant some seeds** or bulbs, or perhaps a seedling or young plant –

an antidote to the temptation to see your garden as merely a place that requires endless maintenance in the form of weeding, pruning and chopping back. Being able to see something of your own making (or at least facilitating) grow to maturity is one of the privileges of being human. And in nourishing these growing things we learn to still the distractions of the ego.

585   **Make a Zen garden** in a little sandpit with artfully placed rocks. Rake the sand around the rocks. Meditate on the beautiful pattern you have created. (Use gravel, if you wish, as a low-maintenance alternative to sand.)

Or make **an indoor version (586)** inside a shallow container, perhaps on the kitchen windowsill. Use an old kitchen fork to rake the sand.

587   **Plant a herbal peace garden**, perhaps positioning clumps of herbs to make the shape of a dove, a heart, or some other symbolic device.

588   **Grow your own vegetables.** This brings a double pleasure: a degree of self-sufficiency, combined with the joy of giving away any surplus to family, friends or neighbours.

589   **Plant a tree.** It's good for our mental health to take actions that require patience before results are seen – even stretching beyond our own lifetimes. If you don't have a garden, ask a friend who does if you may plant one in theirs; or approach the local parks department and make a donation to posterity.

590 **"Age" garden ornaments** by painting them with yogurt to encourage lichens. When tranquility is time-honoured in this way, we often experience it more deeply.

591 **Feed the birds** in your garden during winter, using nuts in a hanging feeder designed to discourage cats or birds of prey. Helping wildlife in times of need is always good karma. If a cat does catch a bird, don't be too harsh on it – the creature's hardwired this way! Also, **set up a bird bath (592)** and enjoy watching the birds splash about vigorously in the water.

593 **Install a water feature,** such as a small pond, in your garden. Cultivate waterlilies on the surface of the water to symbolize abundance. Introduce reeds and place interesting rocks round the edges to create a sense of harmony between the pond and the surrounding environment.

594 **Make an arbour in your garden** or backyard by trailing fast-growing climbers over a simple timber framework. If the climbers are scented (for example, honeysuckle), so much the better. **Place a garden seat (595)** beneath your arbour to give you some relaxing shade in the summer months.

596 **Plant your Christmas tree** after Christmas outside in a pot. Why not deck the tree with lights all year round?

597 **Talk to your plants**. Some people believe that plants respond to the human voice by growing healthier. Certainly they make very good listeners!

YOUR NEIGHBOURHOOD

598 **Talk to your neighbours** and help to encourage a community of mutual support. A network of friendly neighbours offers the potential for dealing effectively with a whole range of difficulties – from letting an electrician into your property while you're at work to watering your plants while you're away on vacation.

599 **Give a spare key** to a neighbour. This act of faith will be appreciated and has the added benefit that you need never be accidentally locked out of home again.

600 **Welcome newcomers** to the area. Ask them what you can do to help. Surprise them with a moving-in present.

601 **Adopt a neighbourhood cat.** There's no need to feed it or even name it, only to recognize it. Whenever it crosses your path, sincerely wish it well ... and wait patiently for the karmic returns.

602   **Take a detour** on the way home, just to vary your routine. That way, you get to know your area, with better understanding of what it has to offer in terms of practical and leisure facilities.

603   **View spring blossom** – a pastime of the Japanese who celebrate the onset of spring by picnicking under the flowering cherry trees. Sip herbal tea with a friend. Write poignant haiku about the blossom. Appreciate other spring or summer highlights as well. In some areas you might go on a magnolia safari during a week-long period in spring. Magnolia trees are beautiful, with open, candle-like flowers.

In the autumn, **relish fall colours (604).** Write a poem about autumn, as John Keats did.

605   **Be a local historian.** Find relaxing fascination in the history of your town or street.

Work

PERSONAL SPACE

606 **Clear your desk every evening** – file your papers away in their proper place, tidy pens and other stationery, transfer hand-written notes to a more permanent place for storage. This may be the last thing you feel like doing at close of play, but it will help you to begin work the following day with a clear head.

An extension of this is the **pre-lunch clear-out (607)**. Not only does this set you up for the afternoon, but it has the added advantage of making it more obvious when someone has put something on your desk during your lunch break.

608 **Emulate the craftsmen** of the pre-machine age by
respecting your equipment. Keep your phone dust-free and your
computer screen spotless. Traditionally, depriving a workman of
his tools was a sin that cried out to heaven for vengeance.
Imagine that neglecting your tools is similarly reprehensible.

609 **Install an ionizer** to restore the balance of positive and negative ions in the air, which is disturbed by electrical equipment.

610 **Put a crystal on your computer.** Crystals, particularly
clear or smoky quartz, help to absorb the damaging
electro-magnetic radiation produced by electrical equipment.
Select a crystal that appeals to you, cleanse it by leaving it
in water for 24 hours, then place it on or in front of your
computer. Remember to cleanse it every month or so.

611 **Tend a plant** in the workplace –
buy one specially if necessary. Check
the plant every day to see whether it

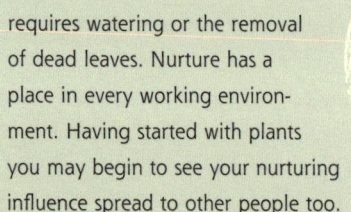

requires watering or the removal
of dead leaves. Nurture has a
place in every working environment. Having started with plants
you may begin to see your nurturing
influence spread to other people too.

612 Keep a bowl of fruit on your desk, to provide yourself
with three things: a source of healthy snacks, a still-life to enjoy
in brief contemplative breaks, and a collection of small generous
offerings for colleagues or visitors who come for a discussion or
a brief meeting with you.

**613 Keep something absurd or incongruous on your
desk** to tickle your sense of humour and remind you that
there is more to life than the stresses of work.

**614 Use a new font or background tint on your
computer** to bring a fresh perspective to your work.

DOING A GOOD JOB

615 **Don't knock routine.** True, it can get you down sometimes, but why not throw yourself into the activity rather than worrying about how drearily familiar it seems? Routine makes us feel safe and provides a strong foundation on which to build our dreams.

616 **Keep a day-per-page diary** for noting down miscellaneous details you need to remember; when you wish to retrieve the information at a later date, all you have to do is recall roughly when you made the note and thumb through the diary until you find the entry. If a temporary record is sufficient, it's usually quicker to deal with memoranda in

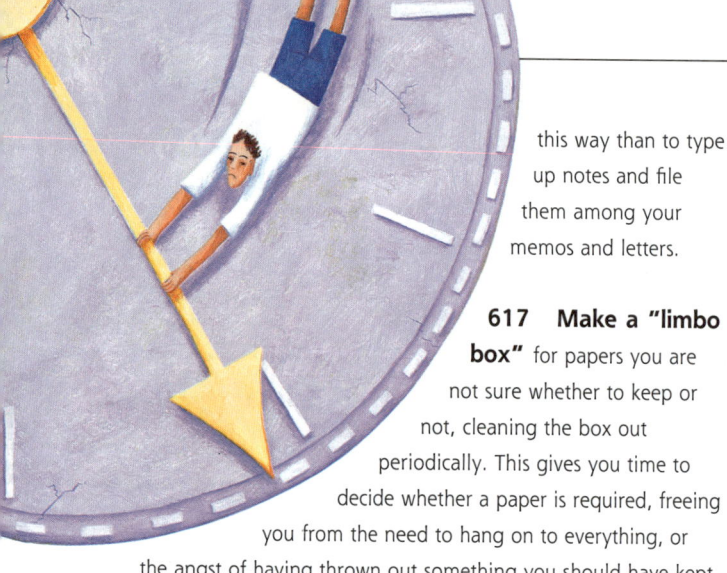

this way than to type up notes and file them among your memos and letters.

617 **Make a "limbo box"** for papers you are not sure whether to keep or not, cleaning the box out periodically. This gives you time to decide whether a paper is required, freeing you from the need to hang on to everything, or the angst of having thrown out something you should have kept. At the same time as sorting your limbo box, take the opportunity to make sure that your **filing (618)** is up-to-date.

619 **Choose one of the four Ds:** Do it, Delegate it, Dump it or Defer it. The ability to balance your work load, delegating, dumping or deferring what cannot be done immediately, is an important management skill for ensuring maximum efficiency. When choosing between options, remember that when delegating you retain ultimate responsibility for the task, and are therefore also responsible for supporting your subordinate in completing it to your satisfaction. By contrast, when dumping, you are assessing that no one need take any action – a decision for which you are willing to take full responsibility. Deferral is the option for non-urgent tasks that you will have to do yourself. Although, in our personal lives, we sometimes view deferral as a sign of self-delusion, at work it is part of prioritizing – a valid strategy for dealing with a crowded in-tray.

620 **Delegate upward when necessary.** If your boss gives you work that he or she should be doing themselves, explain to them clearly and calmly why your schedule makes it difficult for you to take on more work.

621 **Do one task each day that you do not like doing.** There are unpleasant or boring aspects to every job. By doing a

task that you dislike each day, rather than putting them all off, you spread the load, avoiding a backlog of unpleasant tasks preying on your conscience.

622 Complete small tasks adequately rather than perfectly when you feel overwhelmed by your workload. This will allow you to concentrate on the most important tasks in hand, ensuring that they are completed to a high standard.

623 Give yourself mini-deadlines each day for the completion of potentially open-ended tasks, such as dealing with correspondence or managing emails.

Set a kitchen timer or a watch or computer alarm (624) to let you know when your time on a particular task has expired.

625   **Make notes on your mistakes** and discoveries when performing a difficult task for the first time. Refer to these notes when you repeat the task to avoid making the same mistakes twice and to aid you in decision-making.

626   **When making a phone call** have all the relevant documents in front of you to avoid reaching an "information impasse".

627   **Take the name and number** of the person you are put through to on the phone at an office with which you are doing business. This can prevent a great deal of hassle later on if you need to follow up your call with further enquiries.

628   **Carry key contact numbers** around with you. For example, if you are on your way to a meeting with someone, take their phone number so that you can call ahead if you are delayed. Your consideration will be appreciated, and you can enjoy your journey knowing that others are not worried or angry.

629 **Overrule "call waiting"** on your phone if you are in the middle of a crucial task. This will allow you to concentrate fully on the matter in hand. Any important messages can be left on your voicemail. Later you can return the call, free to give the conversation your full attention.

630 **Get to know your computer.** An inability to fix technical problems, or to use a particular function, causes huge amounts of stress. Browse through the handbook to get acquainted with your kit and accompanying software.

Take time to **experiment (631)** with the different programs, exploring the features and looking for short-cuts.

632 **Regularly save your work** on the computer. Get into the habit of saving your computer files every few minutes, and backing up at the end of every day – the stress of crashing and losing hours of work is easily avoided.

633 **Learn speed reading** so that you can absorb the essence of a text without getting bogged down in the words themselves.

634 **Observe self-imposed rules,** even on matters where the company has no declared policy, to build your self-discipline and self-worth. For example, you might choose to limit the number of personal phone calls you make, or cut down your use of the internet or photocopier for non-work purposes.

635 **Cultivate positive challenges,** not negative ones. For example, when working overtime, focus on the challenge of the task rather than on surviving the tedium! Wishing time away makes it lie heavier on your shoulders.

YOU AND YOUR COLLEAGUES

636 Allow your whole self into the workplace. Obviously, work is not the place for letting all your emotions hang out, but that doesn't mean you're expected to hide your true self. Be honest about how you're feeling. Allow colleagues to see the whole self concentrating its attention, during the working day, on the job in hand to the best of your ability.

637 Recognize transference – the psychologist's term for the process by which we project emotions connected with a particular issue onto the nearest available target, usually an innocent party. A common example of this in the workplace is when someone takes out their frustration with their boss on a junior. Becoming aware that you are transferring your emotions onto another is the first step to avoiding this pattern.

638 Take criticism into your mind, as though inviting a stranger into your home. Talk to it. See if you can find something in common with it, a perspective that you share. Use that common ground to build on and improve what you are doing. Treating

criticism as a personal affront and therefore rejecting it out of
hand creates anger and tension, and also prevents you from
absorbing useful feedback.

639   **Let others learn from your mistakes,** as well as yourself.
Creating a workplace in which workers are encouraged to report
their mistakes without fear of reprimand not only improves the
atmosphere but also means that workers are able to pool their
experiences so that everyone can learn from each others'
misjudgments. This results in a more efficient workplace.

640   **Show an interest in others' lives.** This will prevent you
from falling into the trap of seeing people merely as their roles.
Remember, everyone is capable of surprising you!

641   **Be gracious.** Sometimes the people we work with become
so familiar to us that we take them for granted, leaving out the
civilities that make for quality relationships. Remember your
manners. People flower when treated with grace and respect.

642 **Bring tasty edibles** back to your workmates after returning from vacation – it's a good way to spread goodwill and show that you don't push your colleagues out of your mind the moment you leave the workplace.

643 **Volunteer for a social role within your company.** For example, you might go on a first-aid course, or organize cinema trips for as many colleagues as wish to attend. Such activities enable you to relate to your colleagues in a social as well as professional context, humanizing the workplace and breaking down artificial divisions between you and your fellow workers.

644 **Garnish liberally** – or, to switch metaphors, bear in mind that certain work conversations, especially those with customers or clients, run more smoothly if oiled with sociable chat.

   Ask a personal question (645), while volunteering some personal information of your own, to render a professional relationship warmer and more intimate. But don't make it too hot by straying across the boundaries of tact and good manners.

EASING THE PRESSURE

646   **Take an eye-break** every 10 minutes when working at a computer screen. Just allow your eyes to roam around the room and adjust to the longer distance.

Sit at least **30 inches away (647)** from the computer screen and use an anti-glare shield to protect you from electro-magnetic radiation.

To avoid the risk of RSI (repetitive strain injury) in your wrists, rest them on a **wrist support (648)** and use a **mobile keyboard (649)**, changing its position at regular intervals.

650   **Interlock your fingers and stretch your arms above your head** for a quick-fix office stretch. As you do so, lean back in your chair (keeping all the feet on the floor), stretch yourself upward and breathe slowly and deeply for about 20 seconds.

Another quick exercise is to **stretch your arms out sideways (651)**, fingers pointing upward, while breathing deeply. This helps to keeps the wrists supple, fending off the dreaded RSI (repetitive strain injury).

652 **Rebalance your posture hourly** during prolonged periods of working at your desk by changing position or simply straightening your spine and lowering your shoulders.

653 **Do a shoulder stretch** to relieve the tension that builds up after a day spent hunched over a desk. Sitting on a chair with your back straight and chest lifted, inhale and lift your right arm overhead. Bend your elbow, bringing your hand, palm inward, onto your back. Stretch your left hand behind your back and, with the palm facing outward, try to grasp your right fingertips. Breathing evenly, hold the stretch for three to six breaths. Then repeat on the other side.

Stretch a necktie (654) between your two hands if you are unable to link hands comfortably when trying this stretch.

655 **Do a seated twist** at your desk. Sit sideways on your chair and, on an out-breath, turn your upper torso toward the chair's back, holding the back with both hands. Maintain this position for three to six breaths, then repeat on the other side. This gentle stretch helps to ease any lower back pain that results from sitting still for too long. It also helps to unblock the mind.

656 **Cut the umbilical keyboard.** If your fingers are glued to a computer keyboard all day, your hands and wrists will feel the strain. Keep objects to manipulate on your desk: a foam-rubber or gel-filled squeeze ball can be moulded and gripped to flex the muscles of the hand; while a tennis ball offers texture and roundness and can be used to massage the neglected palms.

657 **Break off from a monotonous task** for a while and do something completely opposed to it in character. For example, if you have been silently working on paperwork, have an animated chat with someone. If you have been sitting inside for a long time, go for a short walk in the parking lot or down the street.

658 **Splash water** on your face and wrists in the washroom to wake yourself up.

A **wet paper napkin (659)** pressed against your temples or the back of your neck is similarly energizing.

Alternatively, keep a **water spray (660)** with a  diffuser by your desk, and spray yourself with refreshing mist from the bottle whenever you feel sleepy.

661 **Take a power nap** after lunch – this is when brain efficiency drops as food is digested. Half an hour is sufficient to recharge the batteries – sleep for any longer and you will feel groggy.

662 **Have a 5-minute snooze** at your desk to perk you up if you are feeling sleepy. Enjoy the hypnagogic images that flash across your consciousness as you hover on the frontier between sleeping and waking. Sometimes exceptional insights enter the mind during this transitional period.

663 Seek out beauty in a department store in your lunch break. Large stores offer a feast of visual stimuli. Wander around at random until your eye is caught by a pleasing object or design. You might dwell on something small, such as a fountain pen, or large, such as a four-poster bed. Relish the skill that has gone into making this item both beautiful and fit for its purpose.

664 Visit an art gallery during your lunch hour. Find a picture that is both relaxing and satisfying to look at, and contemplate it for at least 5 full minutes. It could be an expansive landscape, an abstract work painted in tranquil hues, or a religious painting expressing transcendence. Return to work with a postcard of the work to cue the memory of this peaceful encounter.

665 Get to know a park near your workplace. Spend warm and pleasant hours there in your lunch breaks. Pay attention to the

seasonal changes in the vista. Adopt a favourite bench. Talk to the gardeners. Enjoy the relaxing two-fold experience of being amid nature at the heart of the community.

666 **Climb the stairs** at work instead of taking the elevator – or use a combination of the two. Aerobic exercise speeds up the metabolism and increases the flow of oxygenated blood around the body, encouraging the cells of the body, including the brain cells, to work harder and more efficiently.

667 **Keep a healthy perspective** on work problems. Don't take them too personally, or imagine that you don't deserve them. In many jobs, problem-solving is what you're paid to do. Rise to the challenge. Relish the chance to justify your salary.

668 **Give yourself the time and space** to enjoy life as well as to pursue an ambitious career. The Dalai Lama was wise to say, "Judge your success by what you had to give up to get it," but achievement alone and for its own sake rarely brings happiness.

669 **Hang your work role** on the coat-stand each evening as you leave. This simple visualization will encourage you to leave the frustrations of work behind you in the office rather than taking them home. Do this even if  you plan to work at home that evening – it will create a healthy break between the working day and the working evening.

670 **Week off/week on/week off** can be a good approach to a two-week vacation. That way you get four holiday weekends rather than three. And the middle week back at work helps to prevent a backlog of jobs building up.

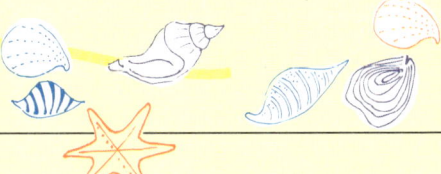

People

GIVING AND SHARING

671 **Make beautiful wishes** for your friends, and write them in greetings cards or to sign off letters. For example: "May your ship sail free." Look out for such wishes in your reading and in the media generally. Borrow them when the occasion arises.

As a variation, you could **make surreal wishes (672)**, rich

in symbolism even though their
meaning might be elusive. For
example: "May your rainbow
never be caged in a pot of gold."

673 **Invent a crossword** for a friend
where all the answers are good qualities
that you see in them. As they solve the puzzle, they'll travel
on a voyage of self-discovery and self-esteem.

674 **Make a puzzle** and send it to a friend – paste a picture, of
someone or something your friend likes, on paper or card and
cut it up into pieces, then send it to your friend to assemble.
Your puzzle might also contain **a message (675)** that is
revealed as the puzzle takes shape – some positive, loving
thought that helps you to express your friendship.

676 **Make a birthday card for a friend or
relative,** using coloured paper or card, images cut

from magazines or other ephemera, and either careful hand lettering or type printed out from your computer. Make the card personal in its imagery and message. Concentrate while doing this on the recipient's anticipated reaction. Anticipating someone's pleasant feelings of surprise like this is a good way to gain relief from stressful thoughts.

677 **Give a thankyou present** to acknowledge your pleasure in receiving good advice. Other possible situations to acknowledge with a present might be: when someone **house-sits (678)** for you; or **drives (679)** you somewhere; or **recommends (680)** your professional services to someone they know. Presents (not necessarily flowers) are also useful to denote an **apology (681)** – saying sorry is usually adequate only in trivial situations.

682 **Give presents for no reason** except to show the value you place upon a relationship. Such presents, falling out of a clear blue sky, often give the most satisfaction – to giver and recipient.

683 **Plan a "royal" surprise** for your partner or a friend, or a close relative. Take care of all the practicalities. Just tell them where to come and when – and what to wear, if relevant. The treat can be anything from dinner on a boat to a visit to an owl sanctuary. Make your companion feel like a king or queen.

A surprise weekend (684) offers the same pleasures on a grander scale. The surprise will act as a catalyst to heighten your own pleasure.

685 **Swap homes** with a friend who lives in another city or region, to facilitate an inexpensive vacation for both of you.

686 **Tell a friend a secret** – one of your own, that is, rather than someone else's. Some secrets are received as gifts of intimacy, and sharing them strengthens the bond of friendship.

687 **Give nice people passports** to visit your private spaces. They are visitors who don't know this "country", so welcome them with warmth and thoughtfulness.

688 **Wink at someone** you know – or even someone you don't. You'll feel in your heart whether the wink runs the risk of being interpreted as lascivious or otherwise inappropriate. If so, don't do it: smile instead.

689 **Teach someone** your special skill – whether it's art or algebra, birdwatching or ballroom dancing, yoga or yachting. There are few greater gifts you can offer. Combine this with the gifts of patience and understanding – and tolerance of a beginner's inevitable mistakes.

690 **Lend your car to someone.** Nowadays this is seen as a big gesture, but a car is only a material possession, after all. Why shouldn't someone else use your car on a day when you don't need to?

691   **Surprise someone** you don't know very well with an act of kindness. A good example would be to pay for an elderly person's shopping next time you're in the supermarket. Or bring your bad-tempered neighbour a souvenir tee-shirt back from your vacation.

692   **Give blood.** Few actions offer such an enormous return for such little sacrifice. As you give blood, appreciate your own health and send the recipient your good wishes for his or her speedy recovery.

Similarly, **carry a donor card (693)**. It's good to know you'll continue to improve others' lives after your physical existence is over.

694   **Drop all your loose change** into a charity collecting box. As you do so, briefly visualize the money doing its practical work of helping –

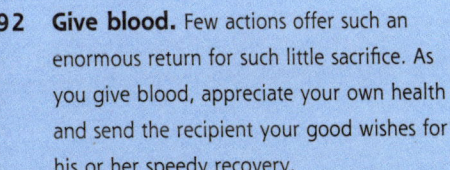

whether buying bread for the starving or contributing to the purchase of hospital equipment. Relieved of the coins, you should feel lighter – a burden has been lifted.

695 **Give to the needy** who beg on city streets – not money but food. You'll be surprised how often you receive heartfelt gratitude. Even if the response is silence, or if the person asks you for money as well, remember that you are far more fortunate than they: you have no right to feel resentment.

696 **Take an active role** as a volunteer: write letters, raise funds or gather aid for a charity. Or, if you are limited by time restraints, you can play an active part by **raising the level of awareness (697)** among friends and people you meet. Your smallest gestures can have a positive impact on troubles far away, and putting this belief into practice gives us a good reason to maintain our level of self-esteem.

LOVE AND COMPASSION

698 **Send out love to family or friends.** Visualize a loved one happily cocooned in positive love energy radiating from your spirit. This love energy carries profound wishes of happiness, health, security and peace. Hold this visualization in your mind for a few minutes. Resolve that you will make it come true as much as possible within your relationship.

As a variation on this theme, wish happiness, health, security and peace to **acquaintances you like (699)**, then proceed to **acquaintances to whom you are indifferent (700)**, then **people you actively dislike (701)**. This is a modern variation on the Tibetan loving kindness meditation.

702 **Hug your friends,** at least occasionally. Even if you're not a particularly touchy-feely person, it's

good to feel the
warmth and generosity of
contact from time to time. If
you're in doubt as to whether a hug's
appropriate, it usually will be – just go
for it!

703 **Give encouragement to a friend** as they
begin a new project or embark on a major task.
To fill someone's heart with courage or resolve
is to refresh your own in the process.

704 **Visit a friend in hospital.** Hospitals, being potentially
impersonal, cry out for an injection of human warmth. Bring
cheer not only to your friend but also to others under treatment,
as well as valiant hospital workers.

Excellent gifts for a hospital visit are tasty **home-cooked
food (705), fruit and flowers (706), essential oils (707)**
to drop on the patient's pillow (see point 466, page 197).

708   **Look for ways to help others.** Anyone who does this actively, as their life's purpose, will live within the gravitational pull of love: service equals peace. Anyone who believes that life is just the survival of the fittest will lead a life of fear: survival equals stress.

709   **Keep your compassion clear.** Whenever you see suffering in others, resist the temptation to suffer with them: it never helps. Instead, disconnect from the person's suffering while remaining mentally and empathetically engaged with it. Disconnecting prevents your power from being drained, so that you can concentrate on giving the help that is needed. This is compassion in action.

710   **Deal attentively with distress.** Floods of tears can be offputting, but when friends or family cry, or even strangers, why not treat the tears as a signal to put your own concerns on hold and give them your full attention? Sometimes tears flow when someone gets an issue out of proportion. But you won't be able to restore clearsightedness without helping to wipe away the tears first.

711 **Put people at ease** in embarrassing situations. Embarrassment is a mild form of distress and one that can often be remedied easily to generate good feelings all around.

712 **Forgive freely.** Forgiveness is the natural condition of the spirit, a petal on the flower of love. When we forgive we are giving out positive energy: some of that energy, at the deepest level, will always be gratefully received and aptly used.

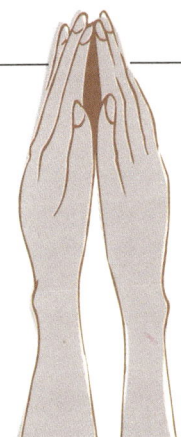

713   **Practise drishti**, the Hindu vision of benevolence. Send the energy of benevolence through your eyes toward others. Our eyes are transmitters of subtle energy, and that energy touches everyone and everything we look at. Give *drishti* to your friends, family, neighbours, colleagues – and to the world.

714   **Bow to the light within the other.** A traditional Indian greeting is to hold both palms together in front of you, as if in prayer, and greet or say farewell to someone by speaking the word *namaste*, meaning: "I bow to light within you." It is a gesture of the deepest respect. Use it whenever you feel that the customary salutations are inadequate to express your regard.

   Other forms of greeting that increase the world's stock of good-will might include: **"Peace to you," (715)** or simply "Peace!" This is a tradition of Muslim countries. Hawaiians use the exuberant, life-affirming greeting **"Aloha!" (716)**. A variation is **"Aloha Akoa!" (717)** meaning "God's love". The Jewish greeting **"yasher koach" (718)** recognizes good effort and expresses a wish for continued strength. In Thailand people give **"wai" (719)** by joining their palms together at chin level and bowing as a sign of respect, especially for age and reverence. The lower your graceful **Japanese bow (720)**, the more respectful you're being. The Mediterranean tradition of **kissing each other several times on alternate cheeks (721)** instantly affirms your bond.

722 **Serve others with your mind.** We can't give physical support to those who are suffering far away, in other countries. But we can help with pure feelings and positive thoughts. Sit in meditation, aware of your self as spirit, connected with the divine source, and transmit subtle vibrations of peace, love and power to those in need of help.

To prompt or focus thoughts of good-will, you might consider the following: **Write a prayer (723)** or **meditation (724)** dedicated, for example, to the victims of a natural disaster or oppressive regimes. **Dedicate a chore (725)** to such people, keeping them in your thoughts for as long as the chore lasts.

726 **Imagine one of the great spiritual teachers** standing before you while you sit in a chair with your eyes closed. They are speaking to you personally. Listen quietly to what they say. You may feel love – or even pain initially. Be aware that their understanding and wisdom are healing you, and their love is cleansing your heart and purifying your mind. Or imagine a **wise ancestor (727)** in this role; or perhaps a **healer (728)** from one of the shamanic cultures, such as native North America.

729 **Imagine curling your index finger around** the same finger of a week-old baby. Feel the soft, delicate skin. Sense how the baby wants its finger to curl around yours but can't quite muster the strength. Be aware of the pure and innocent love that travels through the baby's finger into yours and all the way through your energy channels and into your heart.

RESPONSIBILITY AND RESPECT

730 **Reject blame** using this affirmation: "It is not what you say or do to me that makes me feel this way, it is what I do with what you say or do to me that makes me feel this way." An alternative affirmation might **emphasize peace (731):** "I will not allow hurt to fester inside me. I hereby declare peace in my heart." Or you could choose to **end a cold war (732)** by a unilateral declaration: "I break the chain of blame. I require nothing in return."

733 **Don't be a victim.** This is a negative self-image whose voice can be silenced. Accept responsibility for all your own thoughts and feelings no matter what other people say or do to you.

734 **Keep your promises.** Each time we break a promise or commitment, even to ourselves, we chip away at our claim to be a responsible, self-aware person. Giving your word is a serious undertaking, even on trivial matters. Don't make a promise if the situation warrants a more open-ended response. **Negotiate (735),** if necessary, a looser arrangement.

736 **Be kind and courteous with your family.** It's easy to take close relatives for granted. Perversely, we are often more considerate to people we have only just met. Show your loved ones how much they mean to you in countless little ways every day. For example: **Say thank you (737)** for every action done on your behalf. **Offer help (738)** whenever you anticipate that it could be useful. **Give a humorous account (739)** of tricky experiences, sharing your misadventures light-heartedly. This can be far more productive than making your family re-live your discomforts.

740 **Be courteous to children.** When asking them for help, choose your words carefully as you would with an adult, and remember to thank them and explain why you're grateful.

Also, be courteous to **people who serve you (741)** – for example, store assistants, or people working in your house.

On the telephone (742), many people forget that their facial expressions can't be read. Take special care to articulate clearly and courteously in this medium.

743 **Say thank you properly** – not as a repeated formula, but as a sincere expression of what a gift really meant to you.

Then **say thank you again (744)** after you have had time to use or enjoy the present. Give a report on how much use or pleasure the gift has brought you so far.

745 **Cultivate gratitude** even for things that you have taken for granted in the past – even the food we eat is a gift. From gratitude comes the realization that we already have enough. When we feel that we have enough, we are willing to let go – and in doing so we are well placed to receive more.

746 **Absorb virtue from others,** simply by perceiving *their* virtue. By consciously identifying the good points in someone else's character, you give life to that trait within yourself.

747 **Recognize the privilege** of meeting or spending time with someone who has a keen intellect, or is well-read, or well-travelled, or otherwise accomplished. Don't think of them as superior, and don't be daunted by them. You are fortunate to encounter them – but remember that everyone has as much to give as to receive.

748 **Enlarge the company you keep** by seeing people as spirit, with endless potential, rather than confined within their professional or social roles. They occupy their roles by choice or accident, or a mixture of the two: but their essence is for you to discover.

749 **Find a mentor.** If life is a journey and learning is the path, there are always people who are further along the road than we are. If we value them, we can gain from them priceless wisdom to ease our way. Watch out for such people in your life. Without telling them (that might break the spell they weave!), make them your mentor.

750 **Take advice seriously** when it comes from friends – especially if it's unsolicited. Put yourself in the adviser's position

as the observer of your predicament. Only reject the advice
if you can see a clear reason why he or she should misread
the situation.

751   **Learn sprezzatura** – a virtue prized by Italians in the
Renaissance. It means a kind of considerate, modest casualness,
an unwillingness to put your own comfort or convenience in the
foreground. For example, imagine that you've spent all day
cooking a meal for a friend who's due to visit you that evening.
When the friend turns up at your door, she says she has already
eaten, and would you like to go to a bar? Readily and happily,
you agree to this. You say nothing about the meal you have
slaved over. You are showing *sprezzatura*.

752   **Congratulate success** – even if you believe that the laurels
should have been distributed differently. Congratulations can
be heartfelt – meaning that you don't need to worry about
insincerity – without precisely matching your own assessment
of a situation.

753 Avoid correcting people.
Mentally we often spend energy
correcting other people's
appearance, speech, opinions,
enthusiasms – everything. It's as if
they were a text and we were an
editor. Don't do this. Correction is
unreal and pointless, as well as
being a potential source of tension.

754 See beyond behaviour. We all do stupid things from time
to time, but that doesn't mean we're stupid. Apply the same
leniency to others that you apply to yourself.

755 Don't gossip. Gossip often starts with a betrayal of trust. On
its travels it distorts grotesquely. People gossip to be admired
for their access to private knowledge. And gossip can end up
hurting people. Four good reasons not to do it. Besides, you're
better than that.

756 **Never use sarcasm**. It's one of the lowest forms of humour and makes its victims put up barriers. It's negative and disrespectful.

757 **Learn from an ancient mariner.**
Meditate on the insight gained by the hero of S.T. Coleridge's 19th-century poem, *The Ancient Mariner*: "He prayeth well, who loveth well/ Both man and bird and beast." The mariner brings a plague upon his ship because he pointlessly shoots down an albatross. Regard life as sacred, nature as harmonious. Be aware that if you behave badly, you will not be the only one who suffers: your family and friends will also bear the cost of your transgressions.

DIFFICULTIES

758 **See all relationships as fruitful** – if only because they bring you self-knowledge. Don't fret over a past relationship that didn't work out as you'd hoped: instead, consider what you learned from it.

759 **Break the chain of blame.** Some people are bound to each other by bonds of mutual blame – and the result is usually stress on both sides. Unilaterally withdraw negative feelings from someone you've blamed until now. Remain positive toward them even if you know they don't reciprocate. It may take them more time; but even if they continue to bear you ill-will, no matter! Be karmic: give without expectation.

760 **Ban criticism of each other,** of any kind, open or implied, by mutual agreement: an ideal plan when a relationship needs a bit of help. In other words, go on a love-diet where only loving feelings are allowed – niggles and sarcastic jibes are taboo. Rule-breakers pay whatever fines have been pre-arranged – whether hugs, chores or contributions to a charity box.

761 **Settle a quarrel** before bedtime if at all possible. An
atmosphere of reconciliation will help to induce deep sleep.

762 **Think while you speak** if you find yourself disagreeing with
somebody – or even if you're in accord. Pause if necessary to
decide what you really believe. This takes some practice, as
many people are unable to think while debating: instead they
offer ready-made views. Remember, you needn't talk faster just
because someone else is chattering away – just speak at your
own usual pace.

In difficult conversations, feel free to **ask for time-out
(763)** while you think things through. Halting the dialogue
for a minute or two is a good way to take the tension out of
an argument.

764 **Agree no-fly zones** of conversation with friends or family –
that is, if you both know that certain topics are bound to lead
to an ugly disagreement, just ban them by mutual declaration.
Why fly willingly into a danger zone?

765 **Say "Sollocks"** as a pre-arranged code to impose a minute's silence on yourself and your companion when tempers begin to fray in an argument. This interlude gives both of you time to calm down and be more reasonable. The word is a contraction of Solomon Isaacs and is used by the argumentative lovers in Noel Coward's play *Private Lives*.

766 **Keep a funny hat** in a drawer or cupboard at home. When you find yourself locked into an argument with someone at home, bring out the hat and put it on. You'll make the other person laugh as well as yourself and can then start to resolve your differences in a lighter mood. If everyone knows where the hat is, they can all use it in the same way.

767   Use the power of absurdity,
transmitted through your
imagination, to make daunting
people seem less intimidating.
One way to do this, for example
with authority figures, is to
imagine them not in their uniform
or in their business clothes but in
a **clown costume (768)** or some
other incongruous outfit instead.

Another way is to pretend to
yourself that they are wearing **rapidly-
wearing clothes (769)**, with dyes that are
starting to fade and fabrics that are starting to
unravel. Before the hour's out they'll be naked!

770   Think of aspects of incompetence to make daunting
people less formidable. If you're an expert sailor, visualize them
taking the helm from you in high seas. If you're good at

dressmaking, imagine them receiving fabric, a sewing machine and thread from you and being told to make a dress for a ball.

771 **Reverse the initials** of people's names to make them sound comic – a good way to convince you not to be intimidated by someone. For example, Joan Mason becomes Moan Jason and Betty Wood becomes Wetty Bood.

772 **Try to make an anagram** out of the name of someone who's just angered or upset you – the more irreverent or incongruous the result the better. You probably won't be able to spell out anything memorable, but in the process of trying you are demonstrating that your mind remains free of the person's influence.

773 **Dispel a spiky "aura"** or combative attitude by imagining that the one thing it can't make an impact on is a combination of saintly patience and confidence in your own silent strength. Summon these qualities from within yourself. The spikiness

won't disappear, but the spikes will certainly lose their power
to prick you.

774 **Do a "Joan of Arc".** When, during her trial for heresy
and witchcraft, Joan encountered a question she didn't wish
to answer, she would simply say: "Passez outre" (Go on to
something else). Some topics are not worth engaging with.
Next time you're faced with unproductive thoughts or topics of
conversation, say "passez outre" in your head, and move on to
something more worthwhile.

775 **A medley of leaves.** Visualize your hands cupped and
holding autumn leaves of various hues. The leaves symbolize
the mixed feelings you have for a friend, colleague or member
of your family, or a current situation you are facing. Imagine
that a gust of wind blows all the leaves out of your hands
scattering them at your feet. With the contradictions gone,
you are now free to make a fresh start.

776 Shake hands firmly – not too limp, and not too concentratedly sincere (some people find the double handshake alarming). Look the person right in the eyes as you make hand contact. Let your touch be a two-way channel of good will.

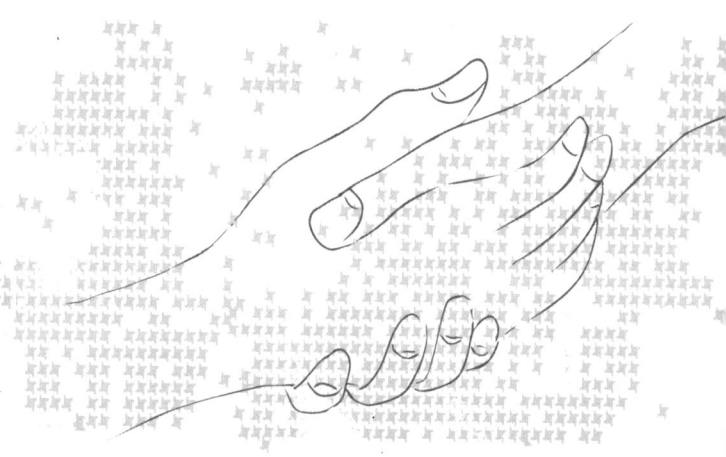

777 **Listen to people.** By attending to others we stay in balance with them. Actively listen to what others are saying, in all your relationships, however casual or temporary.

   Read people's gestures (778), too, as body language can speak volumes.

779 **Ask a direct question** when you're curious or puzzled about someone – but keep, of course, within the bounds of courtesy! Directness is usually welcomed – and if there's something you can't understand, it might sabotage your relations with the person. Not asking questions results in all kinds of missed opportunities – to find out **how you can help (780)**; to **discover the best in people (781)**; to **show that you're interested (782)**; to **discover interesting differences (783)** and similarities; to **learn about the world (784)** around you.

785 **Ask your partner about his or her past.** Even after you've known them a long time, there'll still be much to discover. And sharing memories can strengthen your bond.

786 **With shy children you don't know well,** tell them things that might entertain or amuse them instead of bombarding them with a string of predictable questions. Interrogating a child will only make him or her feel more uncomfortable.

787 **Share the cooking** – time spent working with someone in the kitchen can be intimate, and at the same time a good opportunity to unburden yourself of whatever is weighing heavily on your mind.

788 Take one full breath before you speak in response to anyone. This allows you to be responsive rather than merely reactive; and to fully listen to and understand what the other has said, rather than deafly pursuing your own agenda.

789 Avoid saying "er" or "erm" – it's a pointless habit that doesn't serve either you or your listener. There's nothing wrong with a silence if you need time to think before you speak.

790 When talking to uncommunicative people, ask your question and wait for an answer. Keep an interested expression on your face. Smile through the silences. Something will eventually be forthcoming.

791 Speak softly and warmly for a day. Notice how this releases your mind and influences others to follow your example.

792 Tell a friend what's unique or unusual about him or her – there's no better compliment.

793 **Write a letter to a friend** in a freestyle manner, just letting your thoughts flow naturally and sincerely. You might make interesting self-discoveries in the process.

794 **Record a spoken letter** on a cassette or mini-disk for a friend or loved one who is far from home. **Include music (795)** as well if you like, and **let other people have their say (796)**, too. This kind of gift is part of life's karmic pattern, and will bring you blessings.

797 **Look up an old friend.** Every time we move house or change jobs we lose contact with friends. Re-establish links with someone you miss. Enjoy the pleasures of reunion.

798 **Make up songs** with a friend about each other. This is a fun distraction from more serious preoccupations. The first person starts by improvising a tune to flattering, silly or surreal words. The second person then takes up the tune and composes a second verse. In the process of mutual songwriting you might learn something about your relationship – you'll almost certainly laugh heartily.

799 **Exchange wisdom** with a friend, by emailing each other quotations from your reading that strike you as being particularly apt or insightful. You could do this informally, but it might be more fun to make this a game with a weekly deadline.

A variation on this is to play **angel vs devil (800)**. Toss a coin to determine which of you will play which role. The devil chooses quotations or invents arguments in favour of selfish, materialistic values. The angel's job is to demolish those values using quotations from spiritual literature – or, indeed, any literature of profundity. Sounds serious, but it can be very diverting.

801 **Advise friends honestly,** even if you know you're going to have to say something unwelcome. If your friend has asked for your advice, the stress of knowing you were disingenuous will be greater than the stress of speaking your mind.

Of course, if your **advice isn't asked for (802)**, you have the option of saying nothing. But if this prospect troubles your conscience, again it's probably better in the long run to say what you really feel.

803 **Don't swallow a compliment:** speak it, as soon the thought occurs to you. To hold back on praise is tantamount to undervaluing someone.

804 **Open out self-dialogue.** We all continue long conversations with ourselves, in our heads. But wouldn't it be a pity to waste our best insights on an audience of one? Don't bottle up your best thoughts: share them and let others benefit. This might seem a bit strange to begin with – as if you're letting people into your inner sanctum for the first time. But you'll find that

a dialogue of comfortable intimacy is soon
established, its boundaries tacitly agreed.
As always, giving brings gifts in its wake.

805 **Share your enthusiasms wisely** but
beware of taking up too much of someone
else's time with your own special interests.
Remember, their apparent fascination may
just be a sign of politeness.

806 **Guess who's calling** you on the phone
before you pick up the receiver. This is a
good way to sharpen your intuition. You'll
be surprised how often you get it right.

807 **Learn signing** and work with the deaf on
a voluntary basis. This is communication *par
excellence* – how good it feels to help others
overcome their communication problems!

ENCOUNTERS

808 **Say "Good morning" to people.** Old-fashioned manners
will never lose their value. Smile and be bright while saying it –
all too often good-mornings are mumbled by people who don't
really feel that way. Say your good-morning sincerely, as a
heartfelt wish.

809 **Smile outwardly.** Even when you're feeling low, smiling at
someone triggers the release of endorphins ("happy hormones")
that will help to boost your mood. Try smiling at strangers,
anyone with whom you make eye-contact – you may be
surprised how often the smile is returned. And an outward smile
often engenders the appropriate inner feelings: although human
beings normally operate from the inside out, sometimes outside
in is a worthwhile strategy for enhancing your inner peace.

810 **Talk to strangers** – and not only at parties. An Irish proverb
says that there's no such thing as strangers, only friends you've
yet to meet. With each encounter, try to find one acquaintance,
possession or belief you have in common. You'll often be

surprised how many fascinating correspondences you can find.

811 **A pomegranate, sliced in half,** is an inspiring symbol of life's diversity. Use it to deal with people who think or behave differently from you. Imagine the countless seeds are all the different approaches people can take to life. Meditate on the multiplicity of the pomegranate in a spirit of gratefulness that not everyone is like you.

812 **Bring an open mind** to new people or places, or to new experiences: like a parachute, a mind functions better when it is open. Your way is only one of many ways. Open-minded people tend to find more to enjoy and less to be disappointed by.

813 **Rejoice in differences** when planning a dinner party. Instead of asking yourself, Who's going to get on well with whom?, arrange your guest list from a different angle: Who's going to find whom most surprising, or most different from themselves? This reminds us that it's difference, as much as uniformity, that people value – even though we often tend to assume otherwise, especially when thinking about ourselves. Be bold in your planning: mix rather than match.

814 **Introduce all your friends** to each other. Don't waste any time imagining that your friends won't get on – it's much more enjoyable to get them together and let them mingle. If new friendships are sparked off by this, so much the better! Each friend you have reflects a different source of fascination for you. When your friends meet each other, each of them learns a little more about you, and your frame of reference.

815 **Choose good company.** Undoubtedly, we are influenced by the energy and calm (these are far from mutually exclusive qualities) of the people around us. Peaceful, self-possessed, independent-minded people often allow us to see our own lives in a fresh perspective. And, of course, good-natured people, who like a joke, are always going to exert a relaxing influence.

Be good company (816) and help your friends to be good company too by valuing them and boosting their self-esteem. Show them that you love to let their talents shine.

817 **Take photos** of friends and family, without worrying too much about composition. The important thing is to capture something real and spontaneous about your subjects, and this only works by chance. Don't be upset if some of the photos turn out less than perfect: a snapshot is a kind of lottery, with some happy yesses and many invaluable maybes.

818   **Watch a wedding,** and share in its festive spirit. Celebrating others' happiness is a key stage in training the ego to be less self-centred.

819   **Stay with friends** after a dinner at their place. If it's tricky to travel home late, just ask them if they'd mind putting you up overnight – while being sensitive to any difficulties they might have in this, such as a very early start next day. Offer to make breakfast for them. Value the "backstage" time you spend together, and participate in your friends' household routines with pleasure and a due sense of privilege.

820   **Visit a carnival** if you get the opportunity – the atmosphere can be electric and exhilarating. Go with friends and enter into the spirit of communal exuberance. It's a good idea to take along food and water or fruit juice, and perhaps a portable folding stool if you're reluctant to spend all the time on your feet.

Open-air music performances (821) – especially of world music – can also be uplifting. Scan the program beforehand and choose whatever bands or singers sound most promising to you. Act on instinct – it might be just the name that catches your imagination, perhaps because it carries some personal connection with your life. Take the opportunity to talk to strangers. Mix freely with the other people there and offer your snacks and beverages around.

822 **Help to organize local events,** such as summer fêtes, garden parties, carol singing, harvest festivals, and so on – it's a great way to really get to know your community. Put your special talents to use. For example, if you can draw, you might choose to illustrate·a locally-produced festival program. Be generous with your time, energy and imagination. Everyone has the in-built capacity to be a lynchpin of their own community.

Creativity and play

THE ARTS

823 **Let music fill your heart.** The ear is merely the gateway through which music enters your being. To receive its full healing benefit, open your heart and allow it to be suffused with magical sounds.

824 **Play some old records.** According to enthusiasts, the music produced by vinyl is richer and easier on the ear than the "cleaner" sounds of CDs or mini-disks.

825 **Get lost in a fugue** – an intricate and satisfying form of musical composition. Listen to the piece several times in order to trace each individual strand or voice within the composition as they weave together in counterpoint to form a magical tapestry of sound. J.S. Bach is the acknowledged master of the form – try his *Art of Fugue*, a collection of 48 fugues and preludes for the piano, or the "Sanctus" in Verdi's choral work, *Requiem*.

826 **Listen to a Gregorian chant,** or any other form of sacred medieval choral music. You'll find that the simplicity and naturalness of the unaccompanied singing create a sense of inner calm and spaciousness.

Alternatively, try other forms of sacred song, such as the **Byzantine liturgical music (827)** of the Greek Orthodox faith. This is more complex than the Gregorian chant, with part rather than unison singing, but is similar in effect.

828 **Listen to an Indian raga** – you should find recordings of sitar or sarod pieces in the world music department of your local music store. You can't go far wrong with the work of sitar genius Ravi Shankar. In each raga, a long slow introduction (*alap*) is followed by more vigorous playing accompanied by tabla (hand drums). The effect is invariably refreshing.

Try **Persian classical music (829)** as an alternative, or different types of **world music (830)**.

831   **Pluck a stringed instrument,** such as a guitar or violin. If you listen carefully, you may be able to hear different tones resonating alongside the dominant note of each string. These are known as harmonics. Follow a tone until it completely disappears, then repeat the exercise choosing a different tone. Meditate on the sounds and allow them to relax you.

832   **Buy a pair of drumsticks** and devise your own rhythms. You won't need a drum-kit, only a collection of objects – for example, boxes, cans, jars, books, anything that makes an interesting sound. Suit the rhythm to your mood – if you're feeling mellow, use your heartbeat as a starting point; if you need to release a lot of tension, bang away furiously like the drummer, Art Blakey, performing a solo.

833 **Be a kitchen-sink musician.** The kitchen offers a wealth of opportunities for spontaneous music-making. Experiment with using wooden spoons and metal whisks for drum-sticks, the kitchen sink, if it's made of stainless steel, as a large steel drum, and saucepans for side-drums. Create a xylophone out of bottles filled with varying amounts of water and play them with metal spoons, or scrape a vegetable grater with a fork.

834 **Sing a favourite line** from a hymn or sacred song, over and over, like a mantra. With time the prayerful repetition will begin to soothe your senses, while the message of the text will subtly enter your heart. Use candles or incense to enhance the spiritual atmosphere as you sing.

835 **Imagine "Imagine"** – the famous John Lennon song. Sing the song to yourself and, as you do so, visualize the utopian scenarios that Lennon conjures up. Imagine what it would be like to live in such a harmonious cosmos. Ask yourself what you can do to make aspects of this vision a reality in your own life.

836 **Join a choir.** Singing is invigorating and cathartic. Sing with others and the benefits are multiplied. Join a choir and you'll improve your teamwork and listening skills, experience the exhilaration of live performance, and gain access to a great repertoire of choral music, from classical to gospel.

837 **Apply your growing awareness** of the complex nature of sound to everyday noise – listen carefully and you'll find that there's music everywhere.

838 **Learn to appreciate abstract art.** It's a matter of developing your responses to shapes, hues and textures on all levels – mental, emotional and spiritual. By accustomizing

yourself to abstraction, you are breaking out
of prescriptive categories, and this can only
be good for your own creativity.

839 **Spend an evening at the ballet.**
Romantic ballets, such as Marius Petipa's *Swan
Lake* and *Sleeping Beauty* (both of which are set
to scores by the Russian composer, Tchaikovsky)
are particularly relaxing. You can absorb
yourself completely in the spectacle, as groups
of dancers weave intricate patterns in synchrony
with the music, and soloists inspire wonder with
their virtuosity.

840 **Take to the stage.** As children we make sense
of our world through play-acting, but as adults
most of us turn our backs on this aspect of
creativity. Tap into the wisdom of drama. Enjoy being someone
else for an evening. Take a drama class, or join a theatre group

or amateur dramatics society. Perform for children, or, if you're political, consider using street theatre to make a statement.

841 **Read "Song of Myself"** by Walt Whitman – a wonderfully uplifting poem in celebration of being alive. "Each moment and whatever happens thrills me with joy," says Whitman, and the mood is certainly infectious.

    Write your own song of yourself (842). Rather than writing directly about himself, Whitman uses America as his subject, treating it as a reflection of himself. Following his example, choose a place, landscape or even country that you relate to and use it as a starting-point for your own voyage of poetic self-discovery.

843 **Read a sonnet.** Like the golden section in a painting, there's something intrinsically satisfying about the fourteen-line structure of a sonnet. Relish the words, rhymes and beauty of the form. Shakespeare's sonnets are the obvious place to start. Or, for a mystical flavour, try Rilke's *Sonnets to Orpheus*.

844 **Visualize a poem** in vivid detail as you read it. This not only stretches your imagination, but also enables you to enter convincingly into the world of the poem.

845 **Open a book at random** and read for a short while. Appreciate the qualities of the prose, the choice of vocabulary, the structuring of ideas or the narration of events. Consider those countries where illiteracy and/or censorship are rife and relish the privilege you're enjoying – to be a reader of a book of your choice.

846 **Carry a miniature book** in your pocket at all times. You can buy abridged versions of the classics, or small books containing quotations, jokes or inspiring phrases – great for unexpected periods of empty time, such as waiting for trains or meetings with the bank manager.

847   **Swap books** with a friend – that way, you can sharpen your wits, extend your imagination and test your memory when you discuss the books with your friend afterwards.

848   **Keep a journal of your reading.** List the books you read and jot down notes about them – the characters you found interesting, the images that lingered on in your mind.

   Copy out your favourite passages (849) and quotations. At a later date you can use your journal to re-visit favourite passages or find a passage suited to your particular mood.

850   **Write to an author** to say how much you enjoyed their book – you'd be surprised how often they reply. Ring the publishers to find out contact details, or write to the author care of the publishers, with a forwarding note attached.

PLAYTIME

851 **Make time for laughter** – an instant energizer that stimulates the *chakras* of the solar plexus and the sacrum. The solar plexus is associated with intimacy and creativity; the sacrum connects us to the energy of the sun, providing the impetus for all our actions.

852 **Have a pillow fight.** Playfully bashing each other with pillows is a fun way to release tension – both through the physical exertion of the action and the laughter it provokes.

Have a balloon fight (853) with a friend – a slower, less hazardous version of the same game. Let go of adult inhibitions and surrender to silliness.

854 **Dance a little jig.** The tango may be more sultry, the waltz more elegant, but few dances can beat the jig for sheer exuberance. Buy a recording (Irish, Scottish and American folk compilations frequently include jigs) and leap around your living room like a leprechaun.

855 **Learn ten good jokes.** Choose a variety of different jokes that you can draw on when occasion demands – for example, to lighten a tense atmosphere at a party, to entertain bored children, to lift your spirits when you are feeling blue.

856 **Tickle someone.** The laughter of the tickled is instantly infectious. Tickling stimulates pleasure and pain receptors simultaneously. Make

sure that the victim is enjoying it
as much as you are. And be
prepared to be tickled in return!

857   **Spinning in a circle** is
a popular childhood game
that brings us a giddy
sense of freedom and
release. Find a clear open space, preferably outside on a soft
lawn. With your arms outstretched, spin round and round in a
circle. When you feel too dizzy to continue, allow yourself to
collapse in a heap until the heaving ground comes to a standstill.

858   **Swings and merry-go-rounds** offer us a brief experience of
childhood abandon. Not only are they lots of fun but the
rhythmic motion of the swing and the spinning of the
roundabout are soothing to both mind and emotions.

Riding on a **Ferris wheel (859)** or **chair lift (860)** can
provide similar experiences. Although the heights involved are

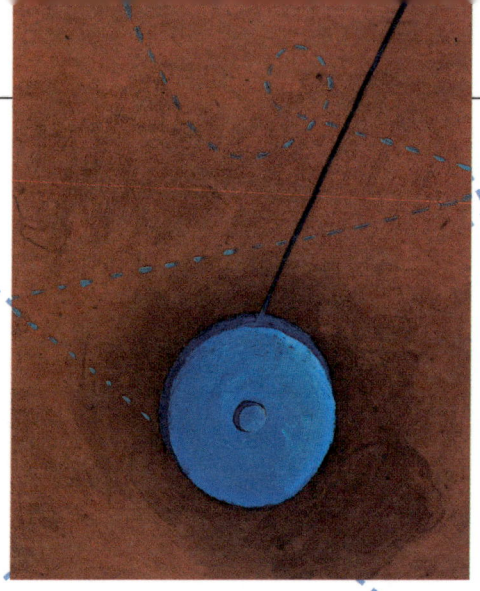

greater (and they are therefore probably not suitable for vertigo sufferers), the movements are more gentle. Allow your legs to swing freely. Enjoy the sensation of being suspended in space.

861 **Play with a yo-yo.** Allow the rhythmic motion of the reel to calm your frayed nerves. With practice see if you can master some of the fancy moves – it's always fun to surprise people with improbable skills.

Alternatively, you may find **juggling (862)** more appealing. Begin by practising with two balls in order to master the basic "throw, throw, catch, catch" action; then progress to three balls.

863 **Cuddle a fluffy toy** – perhaps as you watch TV or listen to the hi-fi or radio. At an unconscious level, this will bring out the carer in you, and as you soothe, you will be soothed in turn.

Choose a toy that reflects your personality (864): a lion might represent fierce courage; a teddy bear, quiet gentleness; an imaginary creature, eccentricity. In loving the toy you will also be loving your own uniqueness.

Improvise a toy for a child you know (865). Choose a character that will appeal to their sense of humour. Their delight in the "customized" gift will make all your efforts worthwhile.

866 **Blow bubbles** to make it fun to do the dishes. Use a circle of wire to catch a film of soapy water; then blow gently through the hoop. As each bubble is released into the room, try to spot the curved reflection of the window on its surface.

867 **Shake a snowstorm bubble** and examine the miniature scene of the blizzard within the plastic dome. Whenever your life seems chaotic, imagine that you are observing the chaos from outside like this – calm and centred despite the confusion.

868 **Perfect your whistling.** This is a simple way to make music at no expense. Discover how to alter the pitch of the note by moving your tongue backward or forward. Keep practising until you get it right. Whistle jolly tunes for other people – it will spread a carefree mood as well as entertain them.

    Practise a whistle of appreciation (869). Whistling is a universal language. Use it for works of art, great sporting achievements, insightful observations, even wise life choices.

870 **Create a sound bath.** You'll need five or six people. One stands still with his or her eyes shut. Everybody else forms a circle and walks slowly around the central person. As they do so, they improvise with their voices, exploring different patterns of sound. The mingling of voices forms a cascade of sound, which washes over the person in the middle. Repeat until everybody in the group has had a chance to be the listener.

871 **Go on a word safari** every day. Whenever you come across a word you can't imagine yourself using, capture it for your personal word zoo. Remember that zoo animals need lots of exercise: use that word at the next opportunity. A large vocabulary gives you more mastery.

Look up a word (872) each day in the dictionary of a foreign language that you can't speak. Sometimes the sound or construction of the foreign word will be pleasing or unexpected – enjoy the fresh perspective this brings to a concept you have referred to many times without thinking.

873 **Read a classic children's book,** such as Kenneth Grahame's *Wind in the Willows* or one of the Dr Seuss books.

MAKING THINGS

874 **Make a paper airplane** and watch it soar across the room. See if you can modify the design to prolong its flight – use different types of paper, or alter the shape of the wings.

875 **Experiment with toy building bricks.** This is a fun activity to do with a child. As well as gaining a sense of satisfaction from building structures together, you may also find the methodical process of sorting jumbled blocks into groups according to size, colour or shape particularly relaxing.

876 **Do a jigsaw** – the more pieces the better. The concentration required to complete the jigsaw will take your mind off any troubles you may be experiencing. Choose the subject of the jigsaw to suit your mood. Rural scenes and expanses of water and sky have a subliminally calming effect.

   Help a child do a jigsaw (877) – it's a very quiet, relaxing activity that you can do together. You can communicate as equals, and you're literally (if you're both working on the floor) on the same level.

878 **Doodle to music.** Spend half an hour sitting and listening
to an album. As the music washes over you, use coloured pens
or pencils to draw the shapes, hues and emotions that are
suggested to you by the sounds.

879 **Draw something with your left hand** – or your right
hand if you're left-handed. It can be liberating to have slightly
less control over the pencil. With a different side of the brain in
charge the results can be surprisingly creative.

880 **Free-associate to get your creative juices flowing.**
Just scribble down thoughts and images as they come to you.
This is a good way to loosen the mind before embarking on any
creative activity, whether painting a picture or writing a speech.

If you're interested in writing imaginatively, try this variation:
fold up the paper you've used for free-association and **keep it
in a drawer (881)**, unread, until a week later. You'll be
surprised at what you read, and will often find unexpected
ideas there to build into your writing.

882 Be a storyteller. Improvising stories to entertain others, whether children or adults, stretches your imagination and challenges your dramatic skills. Have fun with wild and fabulous storylines. Experiment with a different voice for each character.

Play the **storytelling game (883)** – ideal for parties or long car journeys. In this game, the players take it in turns to improvise parts of a story. The first person may begin by narrating for about 5 minutes, followed by another player, who picks up the story where the first left off. The story may incorporate elements of well-known tales or be entirely made-up.

As an alternative game, players could **tell several versions (884)** of one story, from the viewpoint of different protagonists.

885 Write a limerick – a nonsense poem consisting of five lines, of which the first rhymes with the second and fifth, and the third rhymes with the fourth. Traditionally the first, second and fifth lines consist of eight syllables, the third of five, and the fourth of six. When composing your limerick let your imagination run riot. For example, "There was an old woman from Leeds, / Who swallowed a packet of seeds, / From out of her nose / Came a beautiful rose / And out of her mouth grew some weeds."

886 **Write a haiku** to express a moment of insight into nature. A haiku is a Japanese poem of just three lines, without rhyme. Some English writers imitate the form of haiku by restricting themselves to five syllables in the first line, seven in the second and five in the third, but this isn't compulsory. The point is to encapsulate an experience of the natural world, as in this example by the Japanese master Basho: "Year's end, / all corners / of this floating world, swept."

887 **Write a freestyle poem** (that is, without rhyme) of any length to explore any difficult emotions you may be experiencing. See if you can translate your emotions into word-pictures. As you hone the language of your poem you may gain some perspective and a measure of control over your feelings.

Alternative topics for poems include **evocative landscapes (888), pleasant feelings (889), portraits of friends or family (890), interesting relationships (891), thoughts about the future (892)** and **memories of the past (893)**.

894 **Compose a short biography** of someone you admire, whether living or dead. Find out as much as you can about their life and how they have reached their current position. There may be lessons that you can learn from their experiences.

895 **Practise origami,** the Japanese art of paper folding, to clear your mind. Allow your creativity to flow through your fingers, producing anything from simple paper hats to more complex shapes, such as birds and animals.

Extend the pleasures of origami further by building an **ark of origami animals (896), floating origami boats (897)** on

wet-weather puddles, or **hanging decorative origami birds
(898)** or **butterflies (899)** from the ceiling of a room.

900   **Draw a still-life.** Close attention to physical objects will help
you to detach yourself from the racing flow of your thoughts.

901 **Paint a rose.** As you do so, enjoy the sensory pleasures this affords: allow your eye to rest luxuriously on the delicate beauty of the petals; breathe in the delicious fragrance of the bloom. Practise until you are a master of rose paintings, able to create pictures of great beauty that are perfect gifts for friends.

902 **Make a clay model.** Choose a subject that captures your imagination – perhaps an animal or figure. Don't worry about making the model realistic. Simply enjoy the tactile pleasure of manipulating the cool clay between your hands.

903 **Make an ice bowl** for a special dinner. Fill a bowl with water. Place a smaller bowl inside, with flower petals in between. Leave in the freezer. Once frozen, remove the two bowls revealing the ice bowl that has formed between them. As a centrepiece at dinner, this bowl will thaw and collapse interestingly.

904 **Make a compilation** of the most relaxing pieces of music that you have in your CD collection. Record the compilation onto cassette or CD and draw or paint your own abstract art on a suitable square or rectangle of paper to insert as the cover.

905 **Be a Dadaist.** Dada art is a kind of Surrealism based on chance and nonsense. You can take inspiration from this approach in any creative medium. For example, you could write random words on slips of paper, jumble them up in a hat, then take them out one by one to create a random poetic composition.

906 **Learn to knit.** Once you've got the hang of the basic action, you can knit away at speed, allowing the rhythmic clack of the knitting needles to soothe you. Experiment with different wools and patterns. Enjoy the satisfaction that comes with wearing the beautiful products of your work.

907 **Design a logo for yourself.** Incorporate symbolic references to the qualities you perceive in yourself and the values you uphold. Mark any work that you do, creative or otherwise, with your logo, affirming pride in your efforts.

908   **Keep a vacation scrapbook** whenever you are away on holiday. Stick in anything that will remind you of your experiences on the trip. As well as photos and postcards, you can include restaurant bills from delicious meals out, bus and boat tickets from exciting excursions, and leaves picked from beauty spots. If you make new friends while you're away, ask them to write you a personal message in your book.

Keep similar records of **family gatherings (909)** and **inspiring experiences (910)**. Later you can revisit your collections, cheering yourself with memories of pleasures past.

911 **Buy a book of walks,** whether in the city or the country, and schedule a program for completing some of them. View each walk as a mini-vacation. Wear comfortable walking shoes and carry your lunch and waterproofs in a small backpack.

912 **Take a dog for a walk.** (If you're not a dog-owner, offer to walk the dog of a friend or neighbour.) The quiet but devoted companionship of a dog can be extremely comforting.

  Throw sticks (913) for a dog and take pleasure in its excitement as it runs back to you, stick in mouth.

914 **Play pooh-sticks** when walking across a bridge over a stream or river with friends. This is a game derived from the children's book *Winnie the Pooh*. First, everybody finds a stick or twig that will float. Then, from the upstream side of the bridge, everybody simultaneously drops their sticks into the water, before rushing to the downstream side of the bridge to see whose stick emerges first. Games such as this bring out our innate sense of playfulness, which is often repressed in daily adult life.

915 **Take a barefoot stroll** along a sandy beach. It's soothing to feel the coarse texture of the sand beneath your feet and hear the rhythmic lapping of the waves against the shore.

Alternatively, in the early morning, walk barefoot **across the dew-soaked grass (916)** of a garden, park or field. Bring your awareness to the solid earth beneath your feet and the wet grass as it brushes your ankles.

917 **Attune yourself to birdsong.** Learning how to identify the songs of different species of bird is one way to cement your harmony with nature. Practise recognizing the birdsong in a park or garden – or even on your way to work if the route is populated with birds! To help you to distinguish between the different songs and calls, you can buy recorded birdsong with helpful identification notes, or learn simply by watching, listening and consulting a bird-watcher's field guide.

918 Combine favourite things. For example, introduce your favourite walk to a valued friend. Sit under a favourite tree and read your favourite book. Tell your favourite neighbour your favourite joke.

919 Build a sandcastle at the beach or in a sand-pit. Put as much care into it as you would if it were going to last for weeks – though it may last only for hours. This is a good way to accept the value of creativity against a time-frame of transience.

920 **Go on a picnic** – taking a folding table, tablecloth and folding chairs, as well as plates and cutlery. **Try setting up a full-scale table (921)** outside, with all the paraphernalia of the dining room, to create a pleasingly incongruous formality. You could even add a floral table decoration to complete the effect.

922 **Climb a tree.** Imagine that the angel of doubt has challenged you to do so: you and the angel of faith are going to prove him wrong. Enjoy the step-by-step change of perspective and the close-up views of leaves and branches as you ascend. At the top of the tree, proudly survey the land around you, relishing the sense of achievement.

923 **Log-roll down a hill.** Find yourself a smooth grassy slope, lie down perpendicular to the incline, and allow yourself to roll. As you gather momentum, let your body relax. Surrendering to gravity in this way is a small act of faith in the laws of the cosmos – and a withdrawal from thought. Let yourself roll and enjoy the intense sensation.

924 **Make a daisy chain** if you find yourself walking over a field or lawn sprinkled with daisies. Pluck each daisy near its roots to give you a long stem. Split each stem in the middle to create a hole through which you can insert another daisy. One by one, build up the chain to create a crown or necklace for yourself or a loved one – a small token of patience and appreciation.

925 **Design your ideal garden** on paper. Make the plan attractive and colourful. Using your plan as a guide, stroll in your imaginary garden whenever you feel in need of mental refreshment.

Take the first step toward creating this dream

garden by **designing real (but modest) changes (926)** to your current garden. See if you can incorporate elements of your dream garden into your design – perhaps on a smaller scale.

927 **Spend time in a garden.** Nature has been harnessed to wonderful effects all around the world – for example, think of Zen gardens in Japan, or the bulb fields of Holland. Visit such wonders if you get the chance, but bear in mind too that much more modest gardens can be both inspiring and relaxing. Some **private gardens (928)** may open up to the public on certain days in the summer. But why not borrow **a friend's garden (929)** for a few hours? – offer some service in return. There are great spaces in every neighbourhood. Try to spend time in some of them.

930 **Get lost in a maze.** Traditional hedge mazes are usually found in the gardens of stately homes. They are impressive to look at and great fun to explore. One method for finding your way is to keep a hand on one side of the hedge at all times.

In theory this leads you to the centre and out again!

If there are no mazes in your vicinity, have a go at **designing your own maze (931)** on paper; test it out on your friends.

932   **Blow dandelion seeds** from a flowerhead and watch where they drift in the breeze. Imagine that they are your worries floating away into the distance.

933   **Play boules.** This is an old French game, usually played on sand or gravel, involving anything from two to eight players. At the start of the game a small ball, called a jack, is thrown. The players then compete to cast their two boules (heavy metal balls) as close to the jack as possible. The game requires little physical exertion but a high level of skill. It is therefore particularly popular among the older generation who find it a relaxing way to spend time outside, among friends.

934 **Look under a stone** whenever you're walking in the countryside. Choose a large stone that is embedded in the earth. When you lift it up you will be amazed to discover another world beneath – a soil seething with insects and small creatures, bustling about their activities. Take a moment to consider the place of humans in the grand scheme of nature – our world being one of the many that operate on this planet.

935 **Collect acorns** in autumn. Carry one or two in your pocket, giving them an occasional polish with your handkerchief. They provide a small reminder of the miracle of life – that something so large grows from something so small and simple.

936 **Take up beekeeping.** Interactions with the natural world increase our understanding, and honey is a delicious by-product.

937 **Go horse-riding.** Experience the contentment that comes from connecting with an animal. Be lulled by the gentle rhythms of the various gaits: the meditative clip-clopping walk, the lively trot, the rocking canter, the exhilarating gallop.

If you lack confidence on a horse, you can replicate this experience by riding the wooden mounts of a **carousel (938)**.

939 **Work on a farm** to become more intimately acquainted with the rhythms of nature. Why not volunteer your services for a day or so, perhaps during the time when sheep are lambing?

940 **Go fishing** – a tranquil, meditative activity in which a catch is secondary to the benefits of stillness and silence.

941 **Do rain magic** to conjure up some rain when the land becomes dry. Perform the ritual outside: pound the earth with your feet to mimic rain; ripple metal sheets to echo thunder; undulate your body like a windblown tree.

942 **Have a snowball fight.** The breathless excitement and sheer fun of a snowball fight provide welcome respite from the housebound days that tend to dominate winter.

Tobogganing (943) produces a similar exhilaration.

944 **Build a snowman** or a **snow sculpture (945)** taking pleasure in the creation of something so much at one with its environment. As the temperature rises, watch as your creation melts into nothingness through a fascinating sequence of transformations.

946 **Make a snow angel.** Lie on the snow on your back with your arms stretched out. Now flap them up and down to inscribe a pair of wings in the snow.

Evenings

947 **Free your muscles.** For instant relaxation after a stressful day, tense, then release all the muscle groups in your body, starting with head and shoulders, and working your way down to the toes. Finish the exercise with ten deep breaths.

948 **Lift and drop your shoulders.** This is a quick-fix version of the muscle-freeing exercise (opposite). Simply lift your shoulders as high as you can, then little by little drop them. Take a full minute to do this. Your shoulders will probably end up lower than you expect. As they sink, take deeper and deeper breaths and you will begin to feel calmer and more in control.

949 **Be crepuscular** – a word meaning "of twilight". Wherever you are, twilight is a beautiful time of day: the hues of the landscape soften and blur; the lights of civilization glow against a background of residual daylight. Simply hang out in the twilight, enjoying the changing light, or go for a crepuscular walk.

950 **Never waste a starry night.** On a warm, clear night, well away from city lights, lie down outside on a rug and gaze up at the sky – after a minute or so your eyes will adapt to the dark and thousands of stars will appear. You are a privileged member of a vast cosmos. Allow its purity and peace to fill your own inner space.

Buy a star atlas (951) and learn to pick out certain constellations. The sheer vastness of constellations such as Orion, Leo and Taurus is awesome, and once you can identify them, there is something strangely reassuring and intimate about the act of recognition. If you can find order in the vastness of the universe, surely you can overcome earthly anxieties?

Be alert for news of **comets (952)** that may be crossing your skies. Once seen as omens of upheavals in the civic order, comets, with their splendid glowing tails, remain awe-inspiring today.

Watch out for **shooting stars (953)** or meteors. These are particles from space (usually the debris left behind by comets), which appear when they enter the Earth's atmosphere and burn up overhead. An ideal time to look for meteors is around November 17 and 18 when the Earth passes through the Leonid meteor shower – a stream of particles left behind by the Tempel-Tuttle comet. The Leonids are most clearly visible in the northern hemisphere, but can just be seen, low on the horizon, in the southern hemisphere.

Lunar (954) and solar eclipses (955) are particularly spectacular to watch – although solar eclipses cannot be viewed directly with the naked eye, the eeriness of daytime darkness produces a guaranteed frisson. As we witness these movements of cosmic proportions, day-to-day worries can seem less important.

956   Play with your moon shadow
on a night of the full moon. We're used to
casting shadows in sunlight, but a moon
shadow is special. Take it for a walk. Enjoy
the magical glow of the moonlit landscape.

957   Watch a comedy. When circumstances seem overwhelming,
it is sometimes necessary to seek temporary respite by escaping
to the more light-hearted world of a comic film, play or TV
series. Choose a comedy that appeals to your particular brand of
humour – whether romantic, slapstick, farcical, black or ironic –
to be sure of the welcome release of laughter.

958   Watch "Casablanca" on video or DVD – an inspiring film
that upholds the eternal values of love and loyalty, showing how
they can survive the most extreme forms of stress.

   Alternatively, watch **"It's a Wonderful Life" (959)**, the life-
affirming Frank Capra movie starring James Stewart as a bank-
rupt bank manager who, on the brink of suicide, discovers how

positive his life has been through
the intervention of an angel. To say
whether he is dissuaded from taking
his own life would, of course, spoil the suspense.

Watch an **old-fashioned silent comedy (960)**
starring Charlie Chaplin. But remember, no one's
expected to rush around like that these days!

961   **Have a pampering peppermint footbath** to
soothe your feet when you've been standing up all
day. Fill a tub with warm water and add four or five
drops of peppermint essential oil (see point 466,
page 197). Sit with your feet in the water for 15
minutes and allow its warmth and the stimulating properties of
the oil to soothe and revitalize your legs and feet. After drying
your feet, carefully trim your toenails and push back the cuticles.
Smooth away any rough skin using a foot file or pumice stone,
then moisturize using a cream that contains shea or cocoa
butter, or a natural oil such as almond or jojoba.

962   Take a seaweed bath.

Bring some seaweed (such as
bladder-wrack) back from a trip to
the beach. Wrap it in muslin and
hang it from the hot faucet as it's
running so that the nutrients in the
seaweed infuse your bathwater. With the smell of the sea in
your nostrils, soak away your cares for at least 15 minutes. After
your bath, wrap yourself in a soft, warm robe, and drink lots of
water. A seaweed bath has the added benefit of leaving your
skin feeling smooth and moisturized.

For a **more concentrated bath (963)** bring about 1lb (450g)
of seaweed to the boil in a large pan of water, turn off the heat
and infuse for 30 minutes. Strain and add to your bathwater.

964   Add essential oils to your evening bath.

Essential oils are
highly concentrated, so five or six drops is sufficient for one tub
of water. Camomile oil is helpful if you're having problems
sleeping. Lavender oil is soothing for tired or sore muscles.

Burn essential oils (965) in an aromatherapy burner in your bedroom to help you wind down as you get ready for bed. Lavender, sweet marjoram and ylang ylang are all suitable for this purpose (for more essential oils, see point 466, page 197).

966 Wash your hair, massaging your scalp to release any tension that has accumulated there during the day.

967 Change into a light dressing gown and slippers at the start of the evening. This can help you to unwind and means you are ready to hop into bed as soon as you feel sleepy.

968 Listen to the relaxing sounds of nature on CD. Some CDs offer a selection of sounds, others focus on one type of sound, such as whale song or the rhythm of ocean waves. **Make your own nature recording (969)** – perhaps in your favourite nature spot.

LOOKING BACK, LOOKING FORWARD

970   **Write reviews of your most pleasurable experiences.** Depending on how frequently you do this, you could survey the experiences of your day, week, month, year, even life so far. What elements in these experiences were responsible for your enjoyment? Consider how you can have more such experiences to bring greater joy into your life.

    Write reviews of your worst experiences (971). What are the common elements in these negative experiences? Ask yourself how you can prevent these from recurring in the future.

972   **Write a "have done" list.** This is a valuable antidote to ever-increasing "to do" lists, which can trigger anxiety and feelings of being overwhelmed. By making a note of each task you've completed, you'll see how productively you've spent your time, and your self-esteem will grow accordingly.

973   **Close the day** like a file, and archive it. Are there any subtle frustrations or fears from the day hanging like cobwebs in the darkest corners of your mind? If so, sweep them out. Accept that today is now the past, and cannot be changed – all you can do is learn from your experiences. Now is the time for a good night's sleep, a valuable experience in itself.

974 **Plan three goals** (achievable ones!) for tomorrow – perhaps one at work (to clear your desk, for example), one at home (to discuss an issue or concern with your partner), one for your own time (to write to a friend, thanking them for a gift). Limiting your daily goals to three will help you to set more achievable targets, which when completed benefit your self-esteem. **Write your goals down (975),** then resolve not to think about them until the following day. Safe in the knowledge that three of tomorrow's jobs are largely taken care of, you can relax.

OFF TO BED

976 **Learn your natural sleep cycle,** and follow it whenever you can. To discover how much sleep your body needs, get ready for bed when you're tired but not exhausted. Read until you feel sleepy. Allow yourself to wake naturally. Experiment for three or four nights in succession to work out the optimum number of hours that your body likes to sleep.

977 **Warm your sheets** in the dryer before going to bed on a very cold night. This will mean that your bed is toasty warm

and welcoming, enabling you to drift off into a peaceful slumber.

Alternatively, a quarter of an hour before going to bed, put a **hot water bottle (978)** under the covers, at the bottom of the bed, to warm the place where your feet will go.

979 **Drink camomile tea** before bedtime. Camomile is a calming, soporific herb that will help you to sleep. Add a spoonful of honey to sweeten the infusion if you find it too bitter.

980 **Prepare a nightcap** made from milk, honey and a hint of cinnamon. Milk contains tryptophan, which is a natural sleep-promoting chemical.

981 **Take a deep breath** of air outside your door before beginning your usual pre-sleep

routine. If you have a garden or backyard, stand there for a few minutes if the weather allows. Soak up the sounds, smells and subtle sights of night-time. This is a good way to detach yourself from daytime concerns.

982   **Tidy your bedroom** before going to bed. In doing so you are symbolically drawing a line under the business of the day, and you can fall asleep in the knowledge that your immediate environment is well under your control.

983   **Play gentle music** quietly in your bedroom while you undress. It will prime your mind for sleep – particularly if you use the same music each night.

984   **Select your bedtime reading carefully.** Current affairs can re-energize your mind at the wrong time. Restrict yourself to poetry or works of fiction suitable for mulling over as you drift off to sleep.

985   Never take work to bed! However tempting it may be to read a report in bed, this will blur the boundaries between work and rest, making it more difficult for you to switch off from work concerns when it's time for you to sleep.

986   Make peace with the world before you go to sleep with a simple prayer of forgiveness for yourself and anyone else who may have disturbed your equilibrium.

987   Sleep with a smile. Before sleeping, recall or read a joke or funny story. Share the humour with your partner if you have one. Drifting off with a smile induces deeply restorative sleep.

988   Hang a dream catcher near your pillow. This is a native American Indian charm, which encourages peaceful dreams and wards off nightmares. It usually comprises strings of feathers and beads hanging from a circle made from reeds.

   Make your own dream catcher (989) from natural materials. You could either follow the traditional form or invent your own.

990 **Sleep outside on a balmy night** – ideally on a futon placed on top of a waterproof sheet on grass, or on timber decking. Before dozing off, spend some time listening to the outdoor sounds and meditating on the sky.

991 **Sleep with just one firm pillow** to support your neck while sleeping – but feel free to use additional pillows for reading in bed.

992 **Visualize a rainbow disk near your heart,** as a way to quieten your thoughts and help you to sleep. Set it spinning until the colours turn white. Hold the image of the spinning white disk in your mind as you drift off.

993 **Use images to prime restful sleep.** Some people can cue pleasant dreams by meditating on a positive subject – a cherished friend, a much-loved landscape, or a masterpiece of art – for a few min-utes before they go to bed. Choose a subject that evokes calm. Meditate on it before sleeping, and after **waking from night-mares (994)** to avoid slipping back into the same bad dream.

995 **Meet a friend in a dream.** Before going to sleep, imagine calling a friend and arranging to meet them at a particular time and place during the course of the night. Visualize the friend and

the meeting-place vividly as you drift off to sleep. You and your friend may have no memory of the meeting the following morning, but that's not to say that it didn't happen.

996 **The yacht party.** When noise from a neighbour's party is keeping you awake, imagine you've been invited to a yacht party in the Caribbean. Having retired before the other guests, you're lying in a large, comfortable bed, in a cabin of your own, below deck. You feel safe, comfortable and privileged, lulled by the muffled rhythms of the voices above, rocked gently to sleep by the movement of the waves.

Another way to deal with noisy partygoers is to **put yourself in their position (997)**. Imagine that they've complained to you about the waves of resentment that are spoiling their fun. You agree to keep down the aggravation. The best way to do this is drift quietly off to sleep.

998 **Run cold water over your legs and feet** for a couple of minutes if you're unable to sleep in hot weather. Afterwards, your feet will feel cool, and you should find it easier to sleep.

If you find yourself anxiously tossing and turning, switch on the light and **do some light reading (999)** until you feel sleepy. Otherwise you may begin to associate your bed with insomnia, which will make it even harder to sleep.

1000 **Turn over your mattress** once a month. This will prevent the mattress from dipping where you regularly lie, ensuring that it remains firm enough to support your back.

Invest in a new mattress (1001) every 10 years, because the material deteriorates by up to 75 per cent in this time.

INDEX

ACKNOWLEDGMENTS

The publishers would like to thank the following illustrators for permission to use their work:
Debbie Lush, pp. 10–11, 29, 37, 40–41, 47, 53, 64, 69, 73, 78, 79, 84–5, 97, 98, 108–9, 110, 115, 122, 158–9, 176, 177, 180, 182, 184, 196, 199, 200–201, 224, 238, 239, 241, 242–3, 245, 248, 263, 266–7, 288, 310–11, 314, 326, 327, 336–7, 340, 343, 350–51, 353, 360, 370; **Emma Harding**, pp. 8, 9, 35, 62, 70, 87, 92, 95, 130, 140, 144, 147, 148, 162, 203, 232, 234, 244, 247, 257, 261, 268, 276, 300, 328, 348, 352, 354, 358, 362; **Trina Dalziel**, pp. 2, 13, 15, 19, 29, 25, 43, 44, 45, 49, 51, 54, 57, 61, 83, 90, 94, 100, 111, 112, 114, 120, 124–5, 126, 128, 133, 134, 135, 136, 143, 149, 151, 155, 157, 166–7, 169, 173, 175, 178, 183, 186, 189, 190, 193, 206, 208, 212, 214, 215, 221, 222, 225, 226–7, 228–9, 231, 232, 236, 237, 246, 250, 253, 265, 270, 274, 275, 278, 279, 292, 293, 294–5 296, 298, 305, 318, 319, 320, 321, 331, 333, 338, 341, 346, 359, 363, 365, 369.

ABOUT THE AUTHOR

Mike George is renowned as an inspiring speaker and motivating teacher on spiritual awareness, self-management, creative visualization, positive thinking and stress control. He is Managing Editor of *Heart and Soul* magazine and Senior Lecturer at the Brahma Kumaris World Spiritual University. His publications include the best-selling book *Learn to Relax*.

For further information on any of the ideas in this book, you can contact him by email at mike@relax7.com, or you can visit the website: www.relax7.com